500

vegan dishes

500
vegan dishes

the only compendium of vegan dishes you'll ever need

Deborah Gray

SELLERS
PUBLISHING

A Quintet Book

Published by Sellers Publishing, Inc.
161 John Roberts Road, South Portland, Maine 04106
Visit our Web site: www.sellerspublishing.com
E-mail: rsp@rsvp.com

ISBN: 978-1-4162-0636-1
Library of Congress Control Number: 2011921886
QTT.FHV

This book was conceived, designed, and produced by
Quintet Publishing Limited
6 Blundell Street
London N7 9BH
United Kingdom

Food Stylist: Valentina Harris
Photographer: Ian Garlick
Art Director: Michael Charles
Editorial Assistant: Holly Willsher
Managing Editor: Donna Gregory
Publisher: Mark Searle

10 9 8 7 6 5 4 3 2 1

Printed in China by 1010 Printing International Ltd.

contents

introduction

Vegan food avoids all animal products including meat, dairy produce, eggs, and animal-derived products such as gelatin and honey. It is essentially a plant-based diet consisting of grains, beans, lentils, nuts, seeds, vegetables, and fruits. Millions of people worldwide are vegans.

Why eat a vegan diet? A vegan diet is healthy, low in fat, high in fiber, and rich in vitamins, minerals, and antioxidants. Vegans tend to eat more whole grains and are less dependent on processed foods. Therefore, as long as the diet is varied, the vegan diet is the healthiest option of all. There is evidence to suggest that eating a vegan diet may reduce the risk of developing some cancers, diabetes, obesity, heart disease, and several other major diseases. Vegans, however, can become deficient in vitamin B12, iodine, selenium, omega-3, and vitamin D2, so it is essential to ensure that this is taken into consideration when planning a menu. Many feel that a specially designed vitamin and mineral supplement is helpful.

A vegan diet is also more sustainable. Animals raised for consumption use more protein, water, and calories than they produce, so eating a plant-based diet is a great way to reduce an individual's carbon footprint. Globally, livestock farms are continuing to be a cause of deforestation and are huge consumers of increasingly scarce water supplies. Livestock are also responsible for 18% of the world's total carbon emissions. With the planet's population increasing, there is a strong argument that a vegan diet is the only way forward. Many vegans are also motivated by compassion for animals. They object to the exploitation of animals, the conditions in which they are raised, and the idea of killing animals for human use.

It may seem difficult to integrate a vegan diet into a standard meat-eating family diet. Many of the recipes in this book are familiar, however, and have been adapted to become vegan-friendly. By following the general principles of vegan cuisine, it is surprising how many favorite recipes can be modified to suit all tastes. In fact, the substitution may well go unnoticed by all but the most discerning of family members. In general, this book has avoided the use of processed vegan "meats," but they are widely available in supermarkets as well as in specialized health food stores. For the widest variety of specialized foods, try using one of the Internet-based health stores, which will ship an impressive range of goods to your door.

ingredients

The following is a practical guide to some vegan ingredients that may be less familiar than vegetables and herbs.

agar agar
A sea vegetable-based gelatin substitute that can be used for thickening and gelling.

agave syrup
A very sweet syrup made from the juices of the Mexican blue agave plant. Use it as a sugar or honey substitute; 2/3 cup agave syrup is equal to 1 cup sugar. If substituting agave syrup in a baked dish, reduce the liquid in the dish by a third.

beans
Beans have been a vital source of protein since ancient times. They are also high in fiber and complex carbohydrates. Being inexpensive and versatile, it is no wonder that they are central to the vegan diet. A wide variety of beans is available fresh, dried, or canned. As a rough guide, 1 pound of dried beans produces about 7 cups of cooked beans, which is about 3 1/2 (15-ounce) cans (drained) of beans. To cook dried beans, pick over the beans and remove any damaged ones. Soak the beans in cold water overnight, or for at least 4 hours, prior to cooking. Drain the soaked beans and put them in a saucepan and cover with water or bouillon (the liquid should be about 2 inches above the top of the beans). Do not salt until the beans are cooked, because the salt will toughen them during cooking. Bring to a fast boil for 5 minutes (10 for kidney beans to remove toxins), then simmer over a low heat until tender (see chart opposite for cooking times). It is impossible to state cooking times precisely; therefore, cooking several types of beans together is best avoided.

The following are the most commonly cooked dried beans:

Bean type	Cooking time
Mung beans Split peas	35–45 minutes
Dried peas Fava beans Lima beans	45 minutes to 1 1/4 hours
Cannellini beans Cranberry beans Kidney beans	1 1/4–1 3/4 hours
Adzuki beans	1–1 1/2 hours
Black beans Garbanzo beans Navy beans Pinto beans	1 1/2–2 hours
Soybeans	2–3 hours

brown rice syrup

A mild, lightly refined syrup that contains complex sugars, which are absorbed slowly in the bloodstream. Use it as a sugar or honey substitute; 1 cup brown rice syrup is equal to 1 cup sugar. If substituting it in a baked dish, reduce the liquid in the dish by a third. Note that some brands use barley enzymes to produce the syrup, so they are not gluten-free.

carob

A chocolate-like substance made from the pod of the carob tree. It comes in powder, chips, or in a bar. Carob beans are also the source of a common thickening agent, locust bean gum

cheese

A number of manufacturers make soy-based cheese substitutes in a variety of flavors and textures, including hard cheeses such as cheddar and Parmesan, mozzarella, and soft cream cheeses. In general, they have the same cooking and melting qualities as those cheeses they are mimicking. These nondairy cheeses are available in health food stores and over the Internet. (See also nutritional yeast, page 12, and cheese substitutes, page 19.)

egg replacer

A commercially available blend of starches and leavening agents that can be used in place of eggs in many recipes. (See also egg substitutes, pages 20–21.)

fats

The following fats are acceptable in a vegan diet: soy or other nondairy margarine, nondairy butter, nondairy spreads, nonhydrogenated white fat (shortening), and nut butters. (See also butter substitutes, page 18, and oils, pages 12–13.)

flour

Wheat flour is used throughout this book, unless otherwise stated. The following flours are wheat-and gluten-free: arrowroot, barley, brown rice, buckwheat, cornstarch, garbanzo, maize, millet, potato, rice, rye, sorghum, soy, and tapioca flour. They may require the addition of slightly more liquid than wheat flours, so always check package details.

grains

These include barley, buckwheat (kasha) corn, kamut, millet, oats, quinoa, rice, rye, spelt, and wheat berry. They form the backbone of the vegan diets and are either cooked whole or as a flour. To cook them whole, put in lightly salted boiling water, reduce the heat to a simmer, and cook until tender. Cooking time can take from 15 minutes for rice to 2 hours.

honey

Honey is an animal-derived product and as such is not vegan. There are several good syrup substitution options, including agave, brown rice, corn, fruit, and maple syrups. The different syrups have very different sugar levels per teaspoon, so check the labels.

lentils

Lentils are legumes. They are low in fat and high in protein and fiber, and they are a vegan staple. Red, green, and brown lentils are the most commonly used, but Asian markets and health stores offer a wider range. Always pick over lentils to remove stray stones or broken lentils before cooking, then rinse in cold water.

To cook lentils, use 3 cups water or bouillon to 1 cup lentils. Add flavorings such as herbs, garlic, and onions to the liquid in the pan, but do not add salt until the lentils are soft. Bring the liquid to a boil, add the lentils, boil rapidly for 2–3 minutes, then simmer until tender. Cooking time varies from about 15 minutes for red lentils to about 20–25 minutes for other types. If using lentils in salads, drain as soon as they are tender; for purées, soups, and stews, a slightly softer texture is better.

Brown lentils	Plumper than green lentils, can become mushy if overcooked, good for soups
French green lentils (puy lentils)	Retain their shape after cooking, good in salads and stews
Green lentils	A large flat lentil that holds its shape well, good in soups and salads
Red lentils	Become mushy if overcooked, good in soups, stews, and purées

maple syrup

Derived from the sap of the maple tree, maple syrup has a wonderful rich, tonal flavor. Do not confuse it with "maple-flavored" pancake syrups. To use maple syrup in place of sugar, use 3/4 cup maple syrup for every 1 cup sugar. Reduce liquid in baked recipes by a quarter.

mycoprotein

A low-fat, meat-free protein whose principle ingredient is a form of fungus. Beware, most varieties contain small quantities of egg, so they are not vegan.

nutritional yeast

Don't be put off by its fish food-like appearance. Nutritional yeast has a strong, almost cheese-like flavor and is great as a Parmesan cheese substitute. It also adds a depth of flavor to any soup or stew that is in need of a little oomph. Do not confuse it with brewer's yeast, as they are not the same thing. Purchase in health food stores or gourmet food stores.

nuts

Nuts are a good source of protein and fiber. Almonds, cashew, macadamia, peanuts, pecans, and walnuts are great cupboard staples. Store in a cool, dark place, or in the freezer.

oils

Extra-virgin olive oil is a good choice where its fantastic flavor has a chance to shine through such as in stir-fries and salads. However, where the oil facilitates cooking or in baking, subtle-flavored oils such as sunflower, safflower, or canola oils are best. In general, avoid vegetable oil. This is usually hydrogenated, which results in higher trans fat levels (the bad cholesterols). Nut oils are great in gourmet cooking. Experiment with them in salad dressings or sprinkle them on freshly cooked vegetables. Peanut oil, in particular, has gained in popularity and is particularly good for stir-frying because of its high heat tolerance.

Sesame oil is good for flavor, especially in Asian dishes. Because its chemistry, flax oil should not be used in cooking; however, it is high in omega-3 fatty acids and can be used in place of fish oils in the diet. Use it in place of butter on dishes such as popcorn and steamed vegetables.

phyllo dough
This dough is vegan and perfect for making quick and impressive pastries. It comes packaged, either fresh or frozen, in bundles of sheets most commonly 12x17 inches. It is best to defrost phyllo slowly, use it at room temperature, and to work with it quickly, keeping the sheets covered with a clean damp cloth to prevent them from drying out.

seitan
Seitan is made from wheat gluten and is a good source of protein. It may be made at home by removing starch from glutenous wheat flour, but is more commonly purchased from the refrigerated section of health food stores. Its resemblance to meat in both appearance and texture makes it a popular meat substitute. It is the basis for many meat-alternative products.

sugar
White sugar may or may not be vegan. It is made from both cane and beet sugar. Cane sugar is refined by filtering through charcoal; in some factories this may be derived from cow bones. Beet sugar does not require charcoal filtering as part of the refining process, so it is animal-free. Some vegans avoid commercial white sugar entirely by substituting raw sugar or unbleached cane sugar, available in health stores. Vegan, organic, powdered sugar is available but hard to find; however, you can make your own confectioners' sugar by processing 2 cups granulated sugar with 2 tablespoons cornstarch on high power in the food processor. Brown sugar may be refined or unrefined; its brown coloring is due to the presence of molasses. Demerara and muscavado are brown sugars derived from evaporated cane juice, so they avoid the filtering process.

tempeh

Tempeh is fermented soybean cake. It may be marinated, sautéed, broiled, grilled, or baked. It can also be crumbled and used as a ground meat substitute in dishes such as chili.

texturized vegetable protein (TVP)

TVP is made from defatted soy flour, a by-product of the extraction of soybean oil, hence it is also known as soy protein. It is high in protein but low in fat. TVP comes in small dry chunks resembling dried vegetables, or in a ground form. Because of its varying texture and flavorless quality, TVP is manufactured to mimic meat in the form of ground beef and chicken fillets, for instance. It is often used in chili, tacos, veggie burgers, stews, curries, and soups.

tofu

Tofu is a soybean curd available in several textures and an increasing number of flavors. Being high in protein, it is a staple of the vegan diet. Firm and extra-firm tofu hold their shape, absorb flavors well, and can be diced or cut into slices, then sautéed, broiled, grilled, or baked. Press firm and extra-firm tofu to remove excess liquid. Put in a colander atop a bowl, put a plate over the tofu, and weight down with a can. Leave for a minimum of 20 minutes, or overnight. Tofu may be frozen to alter its texture. The result is a chewier, more "meaty" tofu with a sponginess that enables it to soak up more flavor when marinated. Defrost completely before use. Silken or soft tofu has a custard-like texture and a mild creamy flavor. It is excellent in desserts, sauces, dressings, and as an addition to soups and stews.

yogurt

Soy yogurt is available plain and in a range of flavors. The brands vary in taste and texture, so test the market for your favorite.

animal-free substitutes

There are a number of options for substituting non-vegan products in the diet.

milk substitutes

The most commonly used nondairy milk is soy milk, but oat milk, almond milk, and rice milk are also easily available. All may be used in cooking and in beverages. Nondairy milks are usually sold in the refrigerated section of most grocery stores and in nonrefrigerated, boxed form on the shelves. Nondairy milks are available in vanilla and chocolate flavors; always check the package to be sure the flavored milk is vegan. Always seek the advice of a health professional before using nondairy milks for infants.

Almond milk: A lightly sweet milk good for cereals, beverages, desserts, and baking. Contains high levels of vitamin A and other vitamins and minerals and omega fatty acids, but is lower in protein than soy milk. Most are not soy-free because they use soy lecithin. Almond milk is free of cholesterol and saturated fat.

homemade almond milk

1 cup raw almonds
1 tbsp. brown rice syrup

4 cups water
pinch salt

Blend the ingredients in a blender until creamy and smooth. Pour through a fine mesh bag or a cheesecloth into a bowl, squeezing the bag to force through all the liquid. Chill.
Makes 1 quart

Coconut milk: A sweet milk naturally found in the heart of the coconut. Rarely available fresh, most varieties are made by squeezing the liquid out of coconut flesh and then adding water. Coconut milk is high in saturated fat but low in calories and protein.

homemade coconut milk

1 1/2 cups shredded coconut

3 cups hot (not boiling) water

Combine the coconut and water in a bowl; cool to room temperature. Pour through a fine mesh bag or a cheesecloth into a bowl, squeezing the bag to force through all the liquid. Chill. *Makes 2 1/2 cups*

Oat milk: Of the nondairy milks, oat milk performs best at higher temperatures, especially in soups and stews. It will reduce and thicken slightly. It is cholesterol-free. Note that not all brands are gluten-free.

homemade oat milk

1 cup oats (not quick-cooking)
5 cups water
1/2 tsp. vanilla extract
pinch ground nutmeg

1 tsp. cornstarch
1 tbsp. raw sugar
pinch salt

Combine the ingredients in a pan. Bring to a boil over a medium-high heat, reduce the heat, cover, and simmer until the oats are well cooked, approximately 10 minutes. Cool, then put in a blender, and blend until smooth; let stand for 1 hour. Pour through a fine mesh bag or a cheesecloth into a bowl, squeezing the bag to force through all the liquid. Chill. *Makes 1 quart*

Rice milk: Thinner and sweeter than soy milk and higher in carbohydrates than cow's milk. Rice milk is also cholesterol-free and saturated fat-free. Rice milk is good on cereals and in beverages. It does not perform well in cooking without the use of stabilizers. Available fortified with calcium and vitamins A and D.

4 cups water
1/2 tsp. vanilla extract

1/2 cup brown or white rice

Combine the ingredients in a pan. Bring to a boil over a medium-high heat, reduce the heat, cover, and simmer until the rice is very soft, about 25 minutes. Cool, then put in a blender and blend until smooth; let stand for 1 hour. Pour through a fine mesh bag or a cheesecloth into a bowl, squeezing the bag to force through all the liquid. Chill.
Makes 2 1/2 cups

Soy milk: Rich, higher in fat, fiber, and protein than most nondairy milks and probably the best all-round dairy milk substitute. It cooks well due to its stability at high temperatures. However, its taste is less successful in some delicate sweet dishes. Soy milk is cholesterol-free and saturated fat-free, but it has a high concentration of omega-3 fatty acids.

cream substitutes
Soy cream is available on the supermarket shelves alongside soy milk. Nondairy sour cream is available in a more limited number of outlets and is found with the chilled foods. Mass market nondairy creamers are lactose-free but are not nondairy products because they tend to be made from casein, a protein-rich milk derivative. Look for soy-based creamers.

nondairy half-and-half

1/2 cup soy milk
2 tsp. cornstarch
1–2 tsp. vanilla extract

5 tbsp. superfine sugar
1/3 cup canola oil

Put the soy milk, sugar, and cornstarch in a blender. Blend on a low speed and very, very slowly pour in the oil. Flavor with vanilla extract to taste. Chill until thickened.
Makes scant 1 cup

nondairy whipped cream

8 oz. firm tofu, drained   **2 tsp. brown rice syrup**
few drops vanilla extract

Blend the ingredients in a blender until creamy and smooth.
Makes 1 cup

nondairy sour cream

8 oz. firm tofu, drained   **1/4 cup canola or sunflower oil**
2 tbsp. lemon juice   **1/2 tsp. salt**

Blend the ingredients in a blender until creamy and smooth.
Makes 1 1/4 cups

butter substitutes

Margarine is the best substitute for butter, particularly in baking. However, not all commercial brands are vegan. Many contain some whey or lactose and many contain unhealthy hydrogenated oils. Soy margarine is a sound choice, but in general, look for margarines that contain no trans fats or hydrogenated oils. Solid margarines (but not margarine spreads) can be successfully substituted for butter in most situations.

Shortening is the other alternative. This is a vegetable-based fat with a higher smoke point than margarine or butter, making it ideal for cooking at high temperatures, such as deep-frying. Shortening is 100% fat, as opposed to margarine, which is typically 80%. This makes it good for use in pastry and shortbreads because the higher the fat content, the shorter, or crumblier, the texture of the finished pastry. Solid fats also act as a leavening agent, helping cakes and biscuits to rise. Buttery spreads and soft margarines have a lower fat content than margarine or shortening, typically around 60%. Low-fat versions, however, may contain only 40% fat and are less successful for baking purposes, because the leavening, tenderizing, and crisping properties are reduced.

cheese substitutes

A wide variety of nondairy cheese is available in health food and gourmet shops. Cheddar, Monterey Jack, mozzarella, and soft cream cheese are relatively easy to find and should be cooked as their dairy counterparts. Nondairy Parmesan is available too, but sprinkling a small quantity of nutritional yeast on food in place of Parmesan is a great substitute too. Some vegetarian cheeses may still contain small amounts of animal product using whey, rennet, or casein, so always check that soy-based cheese substitutes are suitable for vegans.

mock parmesan

1/4 cup nutritional yeast   1/4 cup sesame seeds, toasted
1/4 tsp. salt

Process the ingredients in a blender until completely ground. Note that some people prefer to use blanched almonds in place of sesame seeds.
Makes 1/2 cup

nondairy cream cheese

1/4 cup raw cashews   1 cup silken tofu, well drained
1–2 tbsp. soy milk   1 tbsp. brown rice or agave syrup
1 tsp. salt   1/2 tsp. white pepper

Put the cashews in boiling water; leave for at least 1 hour, then drain. Blend all the ingredients in a food processor until smooth. Taste and adjust the flavor, adding more salt or syrup depending on the end use. Refrigerate overnight, then use within 5 days.
Makes approximately 1 1/4 cups

mayonnaise

Dairy-free mayo is available in the gourmet or health store, but try making your own.

nondairy mayonnaise

2 tbsp. egg replacer
4 tbsp. water
pinch salt
1 1/2 tsp. vinegar or lemon juice

1 tsp. sugar
2 tsp. dry mustard
1/2 cup sunflower oil
1/2 cup olive oil

In a blender or food processor, combine egg replacer and water and whisk with a fork until frothy. Add the salt, vinegar or lemon juice, sugar, and the dry mustard, then blend on a low speed. Very, very slowly pour in the oils in a thin drizzle. Chill until thickened.
Makes about 1 1/2 cups

egg substitutes

A number of ingredients can be used in place of eggs depending on the function of the egg within the recipe. In general, eggs are used as a binder or as a rising agent. Tofu is a good substitute for eggs in dishes such as quiches or scrambled eggs or when eggs are required to bind. Silken tofu can be used in custards. For binding purposes, also try using tomato paste, mashed potatoes, cornstarch or flour, mashed tofu, or a little bouillon. For rising purposes, a commercial egg replacer, consisting of starches and leavening agents, can be bought in health stores. Follow the package directions for rehydration. You can also make an egg replacer at home in a large batch.

egg replacer

2 1/2 cups arrowroot powder, tapioca starch, or potato flour
1/2 cup baking powder
1 tbsp. guar gum powder or xanthan gum powder

Combine the ingredients in an airtight container and shake vigorously to thoroughly mix. To replace 1 egg, combine 1 1/2 teaspoons egg replacer, 1 tablespoon canola oil, and 2 tablespoons water. Whisk together until slightly frothy.

Makes a generous 3 cups

Component	Substitute
1 egg (binding, thickening, sweet)	1/4 cup puréed prunes, unsweetened applesauce, or banana (+ 1/2 tsp. baking powder in baked goods)
1 egg (binding, thickening, savory)	1/4 cup tomato paste, mashed potato/squash, or bouillon
1 egg (binding, limited leavening)	1/4 cup beaten tofu
1 egg (leavening)	1 tbsp. ground flax seed whisked in 3 tbsp. hot water
1 egg (leavening)	2 tbsp. water + 1 tbsp. oil + 2 tsp. baking powder
1 egg white (leavening)	1 tbsp. plain agar dissolved in 1 tbsp. water, whisked and chilled, then whisked again

basic recipes

There are a few recipes that every vegan cook needs to have on hand.

vegetable bouillon

Make vegetable bouillon from fresh vegetables or with scraps and peelings, avoiding root ends, dirty scrapings, and starchy vegetables such as potatoes. Ensure a good mix of vegetables to avoid having a dominant flavor and try to have at least one carrot and one celery stalk in the mix. A vegan staple, this bouillon freezes well.

1 lb. mixed fresh vegetables, cleaned and
   roughly chopped
8 oz. onions, roughly chopped
2–4 garlic cloves, chopped

2 bay leaves
1 bunch fresh parsley
1/2 tsp. each salt and whole peppercorns
4 pints water

Put the vegetables in a pan with all the other ingredients. Bring to a boil over high heat. Reduce the heat and simmer, uncovered, for at least 1 hour – the bouillon should be reduced by about a half. Cool and strain. Use within 5 days or freeze.
Makes approximately 2 pints

vegan gravy

This is a flexible recipe. You may wish to add onion powder, herbs, tomato paste, or a dash of wine, depending on what your gravy is to accompany.

2 cups vegetable bouillon
1/4 cup flour
2 heaping tbsp. nutritional yeast
1/2 tsp. soy sauce

1/2 tsp. Dijon mustard
1/4 tsp. garlic powder
1 tbsp. nondairy butter or margarine

In a small bowl, gradually mix the bouillon into the flour. Put in a saucepan with the nutritional yeast, soy sauce, mustard, and garlic powder, and slowly bring to a boil. Reduce the heat and stir in the nondairy butter or margarine. Serve immediately, or chill and reheat as required.

Serves 4

tomato sauce
A classic recipe used as a base for many stews, pasta sauces, and soups.

2 tbsp. olive oil
1 medium onion, chopped
1 small carrot, shredded
2 garlic cloves, minced
1 (15-oz.) can chopped tomatoes, drained

2 tbsp. tomato paste
1/4 cup red wine or juice from the tomatoes
1 tsp. dried basil or oregano
sea salt and black pepper

Heat the oil in a saucepan and add the onion and carrot. Cook gently over low heat until the onion is soft, 5-7 minutes. Add the garlic and cook for 1 minute, then stir in the remaining ingredients. Season to taste with salt and pepper. Cook for 10 minutes, or until the sauce has thickened. The sauce may be left chunky or may be puréed with an immersion blender.

Makes 2 1/2 cups

dairy-free béchamel sauce
The vegan version of the classic white sauce, this can be used as the basis of a creamy vegetable sauce. It's also good in a pie filling with ingredients such as spinach or mushrooms. For a cheese-style sauce, stir in 4 ounces cheddar-style vegan "cheese" after the sauce has thickened.

3 tbsp. soy margarine
3 tbsp. all-purpose flour
1 1/2 cups soy milk

pinch ground nutmeg
sea salt and white pepper

Melt the butter in a saucepan, then stir in the flour and cook over low heat for 2 minutes, stirring constantly. Slowly add the soy milk, then increase the heat slightly and bring to a boil, stirring until the sauce thickens. Add the nutmeg and season to taste.
Makes 1 1/2 cups

whole wheat pie crust

This is a basic whole wheat pie crust. If substituting white all-purpose flour, omit the baking powder. Shortening is used here because its high fat content makes for a crispy crust, but a solid margarine may also be used. If using for a dessert, add 1 tablespoon sugar. Make one-and-a-half times the recipe for a 9-inch pan. Well wrapped, the uncooked dough freezes well, either as a dough ball or rolled out in an aluminum foil pie plate.

2 cups whole wheat flour
1 tsp. baking powder
1 tbsp. sugar (for sweet crusts only)

pinch salt
1/2 cup shortening
4-5 tbsp. cold water

In a food processor fitted with a metal blade, pulse the flour, baking powder, sugar, and salt until mixed. Add shortening, pulsing until the mixture resembles coarse meal. If making the dough by hand, mix together flour, baking powder, sugar, and salt in a bowl. Using a pastry cutter, two knives, or fingertips, cut in the butter until the mixture resembles coarse meal. Add 3 tablespoons of the cold water to the flour mixture, pulsing until clumps form, stopping to test the dough with fingertips to see if it's moist enough to hold together. If the dough is too dry, add a little more water as required. Remove the blade and draw the dough into a ball. For a handmade crust, follow the same principles, stirring in the water with a knife. Wrap in plastic wrap and refrigerate for 15-20 minutes or until required.
Makes a 8-10-inch tart or a small 7-inch pie

crisp fried tofu

Serve this fried tofu with stir-fried vegetables or with the tomato sauce above.

3 tbsp. nutritional yeast
3 tbsp. flour
2 tsp. garlic powder
1/2 tsp. salt

1/2 tsp. paprika
1 lb. firm or extra-firm tofu, pressed and cut
   into 1/2-inch pieces
2 tbsp. olive oil

In a small bowl, combine the nutritional yeast, flour, garlic powder, salt, and paprika. Toss in the tofu and ensure that the cubes are evenly coated. In a large skillet, heat the olive oil over medium heat, then add the tofu. Cook, turning from time to time, until the tofu is crisp and golden brown.

Serves 4

baked marinated tofu

Given its Asian roots, a Chinese-style marinade complements the flavor and texture of tofu to perfection.

1 tbsp. rice vinegar
1 tbsp. sesame oil
2 tbsp. soy sauce
2 tsp. sugar
2 garlic cloves, minced
1 tbsp. minced gingerroot

2 scallions, finely chopped
1/2 tsp. each ground cumin & coriander
1/4 tsp. dried thyme
pinch each black & cayenne peppers
1 lb. extra-firm tofu, pressed and cut into
   1/2-inch-thick slices

Put all the ingredients except the tofu in a bowl and combine. Put the tofu slices in a baking dish cover with the marinade, and refrigerate overnight, turning once while marinating. Preheat the oven to 375°F. Drain off the excess marinade. Bake the tofu for 15 minutes, turn over the slices, and cook for another 15 minutes, until the tofu has developed crusty edges.

Serves 4

breakfasts & brunches

Just because you don't eat eggs and bacon doesn't mean that breakfast has to be a tasteless affair. Here are some delicious and nutritious treats to welcome in the new day.

breakfast parfait

see variations page 37

This breakfast not only looks delicious, but is also high in protein and keeps you full all morning.

24 oz. soy yogurt
1/4 cup maple syrup
2 cups cooked wheat berries

1/2 lb. fresh strawberries, sliced
6 oz. fresh blueberries
4 tsp. flax seeds

Mix the yogurt and the maple syrup together. Arrange the ingredients in layers in 4 large glasses. First, put one-third of the yogurt in the base of the glass, followed by wheat berries, then top with the fruit. Sprinkle 1 teaspoon of the flax seeds over the top of each.

Serves 4

oaty apple pancakes

see variations page 38

These healthy, low-fat pancakes are a tasty way to start the day and are very quick to make. They are delicious with cranberry syrup or try them with warmed applesauce.

1/2 cup all-purpose flour
1/2 cup quick-cooking oats
2 tsp. baking powder
1 tbsp. brown sugar
1 tbsp. vegetable oil

1 cup oat milk or apple juice
1 medium-tart apple, shredded
1 tsp. ground cinnamon
1–2 tbsp. sunflower oil, for frying
warmed maple syrup, to serve

Mix flour, oats, baking powder, sugar, vegetable oil, oat milk, shredded apple, and cinnamon together in a large mixing bowl. Lightly oil a nonstick skillet or griddle with sunflower oil and place over medium heat.

Carefully pour about 1/4 cup of the pancake batter into the pan. Fry until lightly browned on one side, then flip and cook the second side. Keep warm. Repeat with remaining batter. Serve with warmed maple syrup.

Makes 10–12 pancakes

scrambled tofu

see variations page 39

Tasty and nutritious on its own with thick slices of good whole wheat bread, this dish is even better accompanied by luscious fried tomatoes, hash browns, and maybe even some vegan sausages.

1 (14-oz.) package firm tofu
1 tbsp. vegetable oil
1 small onion, chopped
1 clove garlic, minced

1 tsp. powdered turmeric
1–2 tbsp. soy sauce
black pepper

Drain the tofu and crumble it with your hands into a bowl. Heat the oil in a skillet over a medium heat and gently fry the onion and garlic until softened, 4–5 minutes. Add the turmeric, then stir in the tofu. Reduce the heat slightly and season with soy sauce and black pepper to taste. Serve hot.

Serves 4

french toast

see variations page 40

Use your favorite bread in this recipe. Whole wheat bread is good and healthy while challah or brioche makes your French toast light and airy.

2 tbsp. silken tofu
1 cup oat or soy milk
1 tbsp. nutritional yeast
1 tbsp. sugar
1 tsp. vanilla extract
1/2 tsp. ground cinnamon

pinch ground nutmeg
canola oil or nondairy butter, for frying
8 slices bread
warmed maple syrup, to serve

In a medium bowl, blend the tofu to a paste with a little of the oat or soy milk. When smooth, add the remaining milk, nutritional yeast, sugar, vanilla, cinnamon, and nutmeg.

Lightly oil a large skillet or griddle with canola oil or nondairy butter. Dip the bread slices into the mixture, covering both sides. Cook over medium-low heat, flipping once, until golden on both sides. Cut into triangles and serve with warmed maple syrup.

Serves 4

quick & easy breakfast bars

see variations page 41

Here's an on-the-go high-energy breakfast for those not-so-relaxed mornings. These bars are great for lunchboxes, too.

1 cup quick-cooking rolled oats
1 cup whole wheat flour
1/2 cup brown sugar
1/4 tsp. baking soda
1/4 tsp. salt
1/4 tsp. ground cinnamon
pinch ground nutmeg

1/4 cup sunflower seeds
1/4 cup shredded coconut
1/4 cup dried cranberries
1 tbsp. flax seeds
1 tbsp. sesame seeds
1/2 cup canola oil
3 tbsp. cranberry juice

Heat oven to 325°F and lightly oil an 8x8-inch baking pan. Combine all the dry ingredients, then stir in the oil and cranberry juice and mix well. Press the mixture into the baking pan and bake for 30–35 minutes until browned. Let the loaf cool for 5 minutes, then cut into slices. Will keep for 1 week in an airtight container.

Makes 12 bars

fluffy pancakes

see variations page 42

What a treat to start the day with these light and fluffy pancakes. Be sure to use all-purpose white flour, because whole wheat flour makes them heavy.

2 cups all-purpose flour
1 heaping tbsp. soy flour
2 tsp. baking powder
1/2 tsp. baking soda
pinch salt
2 tbsp. sugar
2 cups plus 2 tbsp. soy milk

1/2 tsp. vanilla extract
sunflower oil, for frying
warmed maple syrup and nondairy butter, to
    serve

In a large bowl combine flour, soy flour, baking powder, baking soda, salt, and sugar. Add the soy milk and vanilla, and stir until you have quite a thick batter.

Lightly oil a nonstick skillet or griddle with sunflower oil and place over a medium heat. Gently pour a ladleful of batter into the pan. Wait until bubbles appear all over the surface of the pancake, then flip it over and cook on the other side until golden brown. Continue with the remaining batter while keeping the cooked pancakes warm under a clean cloth.

Stack the pancakes on small plates, and serve with warmed maple syrup and nondairy butter.

Makes 8–10 pancakes

orange marmalade bran muffins

see variations page 43

These high-fiber muffins are deceptively light and flavorsome. The batter keeps for at least two weeks in an airtight container in the refrigerator, so make a double recipe and bake a fresh batch each morning.

1 1/2 cups wheat bran
1/2 cup boiling water
1/4 cup canola oil
3/4 cup brown sugar
egg replacer or egg substitute for 1 egg
    (pages 23–24)

1 cup soy milk
1 1/4 cups whole wheat flour
1 1/4 tsp. baking soda
1/2 tsp. salt
1 cup orange marmalade

Preheat the oven to 400°F. Line a muffin pan with paper muffin cups.

In a bowl, mix together all the ingredients. Spoon into the muffin cups, filling to about the three-quarters level. Bake the muffins for 20–25 minutes until well risen and springy to the touch. Cool for 5 minutes, then transfer the muffins to a wire rack to finish cooling.

Makes about 10 large or 16 small muffins

variations

breakfast parfait

see base recipe page 27

grape & brazil nut yogurt parfait
Prepare the basic recipe, using 6 ounces each of halved seedless red and green grapes in place of the berries and 1/2 cup chopped Brazil nuts in place of the flax seeds.

granola & berry yogurt parfait
Prepare the basic recipe, using granola in place of the wheat berries.

wheat berry & apricot parfait
Prepare the basic recipe, using apricot compote in place of the berries. To make the compote, halve and pit 3/4 pound fresh apricots. In a pan, dissolve 1/4 cup sugar in 2/3 cup water, add the apricots and cook over a gentle heat for 12–15 minutes. Remove and let cool before making the parfait.

wheat berry & apple parfait
Prepare the basic recipe, using 2 cups applesauce flavored with 1 teaspoon vanilla extract and 1 tablespoon ground cinnamon in place of the berries.

variations

oaty apple pancakes

see base recipe page 28

oaty apricot pancakes
Prepare the basic recipe, using 1/2 cup chopped, plump, dried apricots in place of the shredded apple and 1 teaspoon orange zest in place of the cinnamon. Orange juice may also be used in place of the apple juice.

oaty apple pancakes with sweet spices
Prepare the basic recipe, using 1 tablespoon maple syrup in place of the sugar. Also use 1/2 teaspoon ground cinnamon, 1/4 teaspoon ground nutmeg, and 1/8 teaspoon ground cardamom in place of the cinnamon.

blueberry & oaty banana pancakes
Prepare the basic recipe, using 1 tablespoon maple syrup in place of the sugar and 1 small mashed banana with 1/2 cup blueberries in place of the apple.

high-fiber oaty apple pancakes
Prepare the basic recipe, using whole wheat or buckwheat flour in place of the all-purpose flour. Serve with applesauce and raisins.

variations

scrambled tofu

see base recipe page 30

mediterranean scrambled tofu
Prepare the basic recipe, adding 1/2 zucchini, 1/2 red bell pepper, and 1/2 green
bell pepper with the onion, and 1/2 teaspoon dried Italian herbs in place of
the turmeric.

mexican scrambled tofu with frijoles
Prepare the basic recipe, adding 1 chopped green chile with the onion and
1 peeled and chopped tomato with the turmeric. Serve with refried beans.

scrambled tofu forestière
Prepare the basic recipe, adding 1 cup sliced mushrooms and 1/2 teaspoon
thyme to the softened onion, and frying until mushrooms have cooked.

sunshine breakfast pocket
Prepare the basic recipe. Divide it between 4 split pita bread pockets along with
sliced tomato and alfalfa sprouts.

variations

french toast

see base recipe page 31

french toast with fresh berries

Prepare the basic recipe, using raspberry syrup or another fruit syrup in place of the maple syrup. Divide 1 1/3 cups of fresh berries over the French toast (a combination of raspberries, strawberries, and blueberries is delicious).

banana cinnamon french toast

Prepare the basic recipe, adding 2 small mashed bananas to the batter. Serve with maple syrup and sliced banana lightly sprinkled with cinnamon.

spiced apple french toast

Prepare the basic recipe, adding 1/2 cup applesauce to the batter. Heat an additional 1 1/2 cups applesauce, 1/4 teaspoon ground cinnamon, and 1/8 teaspoon each of ground nutmeg and cardamom in a saucepan. Serve with the French toast.

day-before french toast

Prepare the basic recipe but do not cook. Place the prepared toasts in a single layer on a platter, cover with plastic wrap, and refrigerate overnight. The French toast is ready to cook the next morning. (Note: This method does not work with the banana variation.)

quick & easy breakfast bars

see base recipe page 33

apple & walnut breakfast bars
Prepare the basic recipe, using 1/4 cup dried chopped apple in place of the cranberries, 1/4 cup walnuts in place of the coconut, and apple juice in place of the cranberry juice.

tropical breakfast bars
Prepare the basic recipe, using 1/4 cup dried mango in place of the cranberries, 1/4 cup pumpkin seeds in place of the sunflower seeds, and mango or tropical juice in place of the cranberry juice.

chocolate-coated breakfast bars
Prepare the basic recipe. Melt 4 ounces dairy-free vegan chocolate and spread over the cooled bars.

gluten-free breakfast bars
Prepare the basic recipe, using spelt flour in place of the whole wheat flour.

variations

fluffy pancakes

see base recipe page 34

spicy currant pancakes

Prepare the basic recipe, adding 1/2 cup currants, 1 teaspoon ground cinnamon, 1/2 teaspoon ground ginger, and 1/4 teaspoon ground allspice to the batter.

raspberry & vanilla pancakes

Prepare the basic recipe, stirring 1/2 cup crushed raspberries into the batter. Also use the seeds scraped from 1 vanilla bean in place of the vanilla extract. Serve garnished with whole raspberries and soy yogurt.

fluffy pancakes with "bacon"

Prepare the basic recipe. Serve with 8 slices of vegan-approved bacon alternative, pan-fried in a little sunflower oil, and patted dry with a paper towel.

double blueberry pancakes

Prepare the basic recipe, adding 1/2 cup fresh blueberries to the batter. Serve with blueberry syrup and garnish with blueberries.

orange marmalade bran muffins

see base recipe page 36

raisin maple muffins
Prepare the basic recipe, using 1 cup raisins in place of the marmalade. Reduce the brown sugar to 1/2 cup and add 1/2 cup maple syrup.

figgy ginger muffins
Prepare the basic recipe, using 3/4 cup chopped plump dried figs (presoaked if directed to do so on the package) and 1/4 cup chopped crystallized ginger in place of the marmalade.

carrot muffins
Prepare the basic recipe, using 1 cup grated carrot and 1 teaspoon apple pie spice in place of the marmalade.

peanut butter muffins
Prepare the basic recipe, using 1 cup peanut butter in place of the marmalade.

soups

This selection of soups has ideas for all seasons and reflects a number of different culinary traditions. Home-cooked soups are simple to prepare, highly nutritious, economical, and oh, so much better than their purchased cousins.

gazpacho

see variations page 60

A quick and easy version of the chilled classic Spanish soup. If you prepare the vegetables and herbs in advance, and keep them in an airtight container in the refrigerator, the soup can be put together in a minute, just before serving. Gazpacho looks particularly impressive served over ice cubes in a glass dish.

2 large garlic cloves
1 large onion, roughly chopped
1 celery stalk, roughly chopped
1 (28-oz.) can whole or chopped tomatoes
4 tbsp. olive oil
1 tbsp. red wine vinegar
sea salt and black pepper

1 cucumber, peeled, seeded, and finely chopped
1 small red bell pepper, seeded and finely chopped
1 tbsp. chopped fresh mint
1 tbsp. chopped fresh parsley
lemon wedges, to serve

Turn on the food processor and, with the motor running, drop in the garlic to mince. Add the onion, celery, tomatoes with juice, olive oil, vinegar, and salt and pepper to taste. Blend until smooth. Refrigerate.

Just before serving, chop the cucumber, bell pepper, mint, and parsley. Stir into the tomato soup and serve with a slice of lemon on the side.

Serves 4–6

black bean soup

see variations page 61

This is a fantastic soup for a cold day when the warming flavors of the spices work their magic. Some of the soup is puréed after cooking to produce a thickly textured soup, but you can omit this step if time is short.

2 cups black beans, soaked in cold water
    overnight or at least 5 hours (or 3 15-oz.
    cans black beans)
1/3 cup olive oil
2 medium white onions, finely chopped
3 garlic cloves, minced
1 carrot, chopped
1-2 fresh red chiles, chopped
2 tsp. ground cumin
1/4 tsp. smoked paprika

2 bay leaves
4 cups vegetable bouillon
1 (14.5-oz.) can whole or chopped tomatoes
small bunch of fresh thyme, stalks removed, or
    1 tsp. dried thyme
sea salt and freshly ground pepper
for garnish
1 small red onion, sliced
chopped fresh cilantro
juice of 1 lime

For dried beans only, drain the beans and put them in a saucepan with 5 cups of water over a high heat. Bring to a boil and boil rapidly for 10 minutes, then reduce heat and simmer for 1 1/4 to 1 1/2 hours until soft. Drain. Heat the oil in a saucepan, then add the onion and cook over medium-high heat for 5-7 minutes or until the onion is soft. Add the minced garlic, carrot, chiles, cumin, paprika, and bay leaves. Continue to cook for another 2 minutes. Add the beans with the bouillon, tomatoes, and thyme leaves. Bring to a boil, reduce the heat, cover, and simmer for 20 minutes. Remove the bay leaves, then take out 2 cups of the soup and blend with an immersion blender or in a food processor. Return the puréed soup to the pan, stir, and heat through. Season to taste with salt and pepper. Serve garnished with thin slices of red onion, chopped cilantro, and a squeeze of lime juice.
Serves 6-8

minestrone

see variations page 62

Long cooking time is the key to this wonderful, heady minestrone. The soup matures with time, so it is best made the day ahead. Don't be off put by the quantity of olive oil; treat it as a flavoring.

1/2 cup olive oil
2 medium onions, chopped
2 carrots, chopped
2 stalks celery, sliced
1 cup sliced green beans
3 medium zucchini, chopped
3 cups shredded cabbage
8 cups vegetable bouillon

1 cup chopped canned tomatoes
2 tbsp. nutritional yeast
1 tsp. dried oregano
1/2 tsp. dried basil
sea salt and black pepper
1 (15-oz.) can white beans
1 cup orzo or other tiny pasta

Heat the oil in a saucepan, then add the onions and cook, stirring frequently for about 8 minutes until golden. Stir in each of the other vegetables in turn, cooking each one for 3 minutes before adding the next. Add the bouillon, tomatoes, yeast, oregano, and basil. Season to taste with salt and pepper. Bring to a boil, then reduce the heat to very low, cover, and simmer for 2 hours. If making in advance, chill.

Reheat if required. Add the beans and orzo and cook for 15 minutes before serving.

Serves 6–8

tom yum soup

see variations page 63

This fragrant vegan version of the classic Thai soup is very light but highly nutritious. The key to success lies in the balance between sweetness, spiciness, and sourness, so do taste and adjust the seasoning before serving.

5 cups strongly flavored vegetable bouillon
2 stalks lemongrass, white part only, minced
1 (2-inch) piece gingerroot, peeled and chopped into thin strips
1–2 fresh red chiles, seeded and chopped
6 kaffir lime leaves
juice of 1 lime
1 tsp. tamarind paste
1 cup rich coconut milk

3–4 tbsp. soy sauce
1–2 tsp. palm or brown sugar
chili sauce (optional)
1 cups sliced mixed mushrooms (e.g., white, shiitake, enoki, straw, or portabello)
2 cups chopped bok choy
8 cherry tomatoes, halved
1 (12-oz.) package silken tofu, chopped
whole fresh cilantro leaves, to garnish

Put the first seven ingredients in a large saucepan and bring to a boil. Reduce the heat, cover, and simmer for 15 minutes. Strain and return liquid to the pan.

Stir in the coconut milk, then season to taste with soy sauce, sugar, and chili sauce, if using, to achieve a tangy, sweet-sour flavor to your liking. Add the mushrooms and cook for 5 minutes, or until soft. Add the bok choy and tomatoes, and cook for 2 minutes. Gently add the tofu and heat through. Serve garnished with cilantro leaves.

Serves 6–8

corn & jalapeño chowder

see variations page 64

Served with hot crusty bread, and perhaps with some mushroom pâté (page 76), this soup makes a rich, delicious, well-balanced meal.

4 large corn cobs, shucked and silks discarded
    (or 4 cups frozen corn)
2 tbsp. sunflower oil
1 large white onion, chopped
2 medium potatoes, chopped

1–2 jalapeño chiles, chopped
2 cups soy milk
1 vegetarian bouillon cube
sea salt and black pepper
chopped fresh parsley, to garnish

If using fresh corn, put the corn cobs in a large saucepan in boiling water and simmer for 10–12 minutes until tender. Cool, reserving the cooking liquor. Using a sharp knife, remove the corn kernels.

Heat the oil in a saucepan, then add the onion and cook for 5–7 minutes over medium-high heat until soft. Stir in the potatoes and the jalapeño, to taste, and cook for 3 minutes more. Add 1 3/4 cups of strained reserved corn cooking liquor or water, the soy milk, bouillon, and corn. Season to taste with salt and pepper. Bring to a boil, then reduce the heat and simmer for 15 minutes, or until the potatoes are tender but still retaining their shape. Serve garnished with chopped parsley.

Serves 4–6

caribbean bean & rice soup

see variations page 65

The combination of tomato and coconut gives this soup a hint of sunshine even on the coldest of days.

1 tbsp. sunflower oil
1 medium onion, chopped
2 garlic cloves, minced
2 stalks celery, chopped
2 carrots, chopped
1 small green bell pepper, seeded and chopped
1 small red bell pepper, seeded and chopped
2 bay leaves
2 tsp. paprika
3 cups tomato juice
1/2 cup tomato paste

2 tsp. dried thyme
3 cups vegetable bouillon
1 (15-oz.) can coconut milk
1/2 cup long-grain rice
1 (15-oz.) can red kidney beans
sea salt and black pepper
for the croutons
3 cups day-old bread cubes
2 tbsp. olive oil
2 tsp. paprika
1/2 tsp. dried thyme

Heat the oil in a large saucepan, then add the onion and cook over medium-high heat for 5–7 minutes until the onion is soft. Add the minced garlic, celery, carrots, green and red bell peppers, bay leaves, and paprika, and continue to cook for another 5 minutes. Stir in the tomato juice, tomato paste, and thyme leaves, then cook for 5 minutes. Add the bouillon, coconut milk, and rice. Bring to a boil, reduce the heat, cover, and simmer for 30 minutes. Add the kidney beans and cook for another 15 minutes. Remove the bay leaves and season to taste with salt and pepper before serving garnished with croutons. To make the croutons, toss the cubes of stale bread with the olive oil, paprika, and thyme. Spread in a single layer on a baking sheet, and bake at 375°F for 4–5 minutes until golden brown.

Serves 2 generously

miso soup

see variations page 66

A Japanese staple, this soup has a rich taste and is quick and easy to make. And, it is so, so much better than the packaged variety. Wakame is a tender sea vegetable that expands seven times during soaking. Do not be tempted to use dashi (Japanese bouillon), as it probably contains dried sardines.

1 (2-inch) piece wakame
4 cups water
1 medium onion, finely chopped
1 large carrot, finely chopped

2 tbsp. miso, dissolved in 2 tbsp. water
1 tbsp. mirin (sweet rice wine) (optional)
1 tbsp. soy sauce
chopped fresh parsley, to garnish

Soak the wakame in 1 cup of water for 10 minutes; drain. Remove the central rib and cut into small pieces. In a saucepan, boil the remaining water and add the onions, carrots, and wakame pieces. Reduce the heat and simmer for 5 minutes; the vegetables should be just cooked. Remove from the heat and add the dissolved miso, mirin, and soy sauce. Do not reboil, because this spoils the flavor of the miso. Serve garnished with parsley.

Serves 3–4

fresh tomato & basil soup

see variations page 67

A perennial favorite, the flavor of this particular version of the soup is enhanced by slowly cooking the tomatoes in garlic-infused oil.

1 1/2 lbs. large ripe tomatoes
6 tbsp. olive oil
6 garlic cloves
1 medium onion, chopped
2 bay leaves
1 small potato, chopped

4 cups vegetable bouillon
sea salt and white pepper
2 tbsp. tomato paste (optional)
2 tbsp. chopped fresh basil or 2 tsp. dried basil
4 tsp. vegan pesto (page 74)
    or chopped fresh basil, to garnish

Peel the tomatoes by immersing in boiling water for 10 seconds, refreshing in cold water, then slipping off the skins. Slice the tomatoes into quarters and remove the seeds.

In a saucepan, heat the olive oil, then add the garlic cloves. Cook cloves until golden brown, remove from the pan, and discard. Cook the onion in the flavored oil for about 5–7 minutes until soft. Add the tomatoes and bay leaves, reduce the heat, and allow to simmer, stirring occasionally, for 15–20 minutes or until the oil separates into small pools and the liquid has thickened. Stir in the chopped potatoes and coat in the rich sauce, cook for 2 minutes. Add the bouillon, bring to a boil, then cover and simmer for 15 minutes. Taste and season with salt and pepper, then, depending on the depth of flavor and the ripeness of the tomatoes, add tomato paste, if desired. Remove the bay leaves, add the fresh or dried basil, then blend the soup in the pan with an immersion blender or transfer to a food processor. Reheat the soup to serving temperature. Serve garnished with pesto or basil.

Serves 4–6

silky lentil soup

see variations page 68

This soul-warming soup is a meal in itself, perfect for anyone feeling under the weather. As an added bonus, children love it and you can sneak all kinds of vegetables into it without their knowledge!

1 tbsp. olive oil
1 onion, roughly chopped
1 green or red bell pepper, seeded and roughly
   chopped
1 carrot, peeled and roughly chopped
1 zucchini, roughly chopped
1 garlic clove, minced
1 tsp. ground cumin

1 tsp. ground coriander
1 cup split red lentils, washed and picked over
5 cups vegetable bouillon
1 (14-oz.) can plum tomatoes
2 tsp. tomato paste
1 bay leaf
sea salt and black pepper
fresh parsley or cilantro, to garnish

Heat the oil in a saucepan, then add the onion and cook over a low heat for 5–7 minutes until soft. Stir in the bell pepper, carrot, and zucchini, and cook for 3 minutes. Add the garlic, cumin, and coriander, then cook, stirring constantly, for another minute. Add the remaining soup ingredients, lentils, bouillon, tomatoes and juice, tomato paste, and bay leaf. Bring to a boil, then reduce the heat, cover, and simmer for 30 minutes, until the lentils and vegetables are very soft.

Remove the bay leaf and blend the soup with an immersion blender or in a food processor. The soup will be fairly thick, so dilute with a little more bouillon if you prefer it thinner. Season to taste, then reheat, and serve garnished with parsley or cilantro.

Serves 4–6

leek & potato soup

see variations page 69

Leeks are members of the allium (onion) family and there is good evidence to indicate that you should eat one portion of this vegetable family a day. Leeks are good sources of dietary fiber, folic acid, calcium, potassium, and vitamin C, and are easier to digest than onions.

2 tbsp. sunflower oil
3 large leeks, chopped
2 garlic cloves, minced
3 medium potatoes, chopped
4 cups vegetable bouillon
1 bay leaf

sea salt and black pepper
2 cups rice or oat milk
1 tsp. dried dill
1/2 cup soy cream
ground nutmeg, to garnish

Heat the oil in a saucepan, then add the leeks and garlic, cover, and cook over a low heat for 5 minutes, stirring occasionally to avoid the leeks scorching, which will produce a bitter flavor. Add the potatoes, bouillon, and bay leaf, and season to taste with salt and plenty of black pepper. Bring to a boil, reduce the heat, then cover and simmer for about 30 minutes or until the potatoes are tender.

Remove the bay leaf and blend the soup in the pan with an immersion blender or in a food processor until smooth. Add the rice or oat milk, dill, and soy cream. Heat through for 5 minutes and serve garnished with nutmeg.

Serves 4–6

variations

gazpacho

see base recipe page 45

mexican gazpacho
Prepare the basic recipe, but use 2 tablespoons cilantro in place of mint and parsley and add 1 finely chopped jalapeño chile, 1/2 teaspoon cumin, and 1/4 teaspoon Tabasco. Serve with lime wedges instead of lemon wedges.

chunky gazpacho
Prepare the basic recipe, but omit the tomatoes from the initial blending process. Use canned chopped tomatoes and stir them into the blended ingredients.

bloody mary gazpacho
Prepare the basic recipe, adding 2–3 ounces vodka, or to taste.

gazpacho with spicy salsa
Prepare the basic recipe. Make salsa by combining 1 1/2 cups chopped arugula, 1 very finely chopped jalapeño pepper, a pinch of sea salt, and 3 tablespoons olive oil. Drizzle the salsa onto the center of the gazpacho just before serving.

variations

black bean soup

see base recipe page 46

mixed bean soup
Prepare the basic recipe, but use 1 (15-ounce) can each of lima beans, pinto
beans, and fava beans instead of the black beans. If you want to cook beans from
scratch, select a prepared bean mix that uses beans with similar cooking times.

black bean soup with chipotle
Prepare the basic recipe, using 1–3 tablespoons chopped chipotle in adobo sauce
instead of fresh chiles. Chipotle is very spicy so keep tasting until you add
enough for your taste. For a more Mexican flavor, add 1 cup fresh or frozen corn
with the tomatoes.

white bean & garlic soup
Prepare the basic recipe, using white beans in place of the black beans. Increase
the quantity of garlic to 4 cloves and omit the carrot, chiles, cumin, and
tomatoes. Stir in 1/2 cup soy cream just before serving garnished with plenty of
chopped parsley in place of cilantro.

black bean & celery soup
Prepare the basic recipe, adding 4 chopped celery stalks with the carrots.

variations

minestrone

see base recipe page 48

smooth vegetable soup
Prepare the basic recipe, omitting the pasta. Purée the soup using an immersion blender or in a food processor.

creamed vegetable soup
Prepare the basic recipe, omitting the pasta and using 6 cups vegetable bouillon and 2 cups soy milk. Purée the cooked soup with an immersion blender or in a food processor. Stir in 1/2 cup soy cream and heat through just before serving.

minestrone with tofu
Prepare the basic recipe, omitting the pasta. Press 6 ounces tofu well, drain, then chop into 1-inch cubes and toss in 2 tablespoons soy sauce. Place in a baking dish and cook at 375°F for 10 minutes, toss gently, then bake for 5 more minutes. Add cubes to the soup with the white beans.

barley minestrone
Prepare the basic recipe, omitting the pasta. Dry roast 1 cup barley in a heavy-based pan for 3–4 minutes, stirring constantly. Add to the soup with the bouillon.

tom yum soup

see base recipe page 49

tom yum soup with galangal
Prepare the basic recipe, but add a 2-inch piece of galangal, chopped, with the other aromatics to the bouillon.

tom yum soup with broccoli
Prepare the basic recipe, omitting the bok choy. Add 1 head broccoli, cut into florets, with the mushrooms.

tom yum soup with snow peas
Prepare the basic recipe, using only 1 cup bok choy and adding 1 cup fresh snow peas.

red curry tom yum soup
Prepare the basic recipe, but omit tamarind paste and chili sauce and use only 3 kaffir lime leaves and 1 tablespoon lime juice. Flavor with 1–2 tablespoons red Thai curry paste prior to adjusting the seasonings.

variations

corn & jalapeño chowder

see base recipe page 50

roasted corn & jalapeño chowder

Prepare the basic recipe, but cook the corn in water for only 5 minutes, remove, and pat dry. Lightly oil the corn cobs with a little sunflower oil and place under a broiler or on the grill. Cook for 3–5 minutes or until the kernels are just beginning to char, then continue to turn until the whole cob is roasted.

corn, kale & roasted butternut squash chowder

Prepare the basic recipe, using only 2 corn cobs or 2 cups of frozen corn and omitting potatoes. Roast 1 small, chopped butternut squash tossed in a little oil at 350°F for 30 minutes or until lightly caramelized, then add to the soup with the corn. Cook for 10 minutes, then add 2 cups shredded kale and cook for 5 minutes.

corn, sweet potato & jalapeño chowder

Prepare the basic recipe, using sweet potato in place of the potato.

corn, cauliflower & jalapeño chowder

Prepare the basic recipe, using only 2 corn cobs or 2 cups of frozen corn and 1 potato. Add half a head of cauliflower, cut into half florets, with the corn.

variations

caribbean bean & rice soup

see base recipe page 53

caribbean black bean & rice soup
Prepare the basic recipe, using canned black beans in place of the kidney beans.

curried bean & rice soup
Prepare the basic recipe, using 1–2 tablespoons medium curry powder in place of the paprika and thyme. Omit the croutons and serve with flat bread.

caribbean bean & wild rice soup
Prepare the basic recipe, using wild rice in place of the long-grain rice.

creole bean & rice recipe
Prepare the basic recipe, using smoked paprika in place of paprika and adding 1/2 teaspoon oregano, 1 teaspoon cumin, and a pinch of cayenne pepper. Slice 1/2 pound vegan sausages into the soup 15 minutes before the end of cooking. (Smoked or spicy sausage varieties would be the best choice.)

variations

miso soup

see base recipe page 54

miso, ginger & spinach soup
Prepare the basic recipe, omitting the wakame. Add 2 teaspoons minced gingerroot with the onion and carrots, cook for 3 minutes, then add 2 cups chopped spinach and cook for 2 minutes until wilted. Remove from heat and finish as for the basic recipe.

miso & asparagus soup
Prepare the basic recipe, omitting wakame. Add 4 asparagus spears, finely sliced on the diagonal, at the same time as the carrot.

miso, bok choy & tofu soup
Prepare the basic recipe, omitting wakame. Cook the carrots for 2 minutes, then add 1 head shredded bok choy and cook for another 3 minutes. Add 1 cup cubed silken tofu with the miso paste.

miso & oyster mushroom soup
Prepare the basic recipe, omitting the wakame. Add 1 cup sliced oyster mushrooms at the same time as the carrot.

fresh tomato & basil soup

see base recipe page 55

cream of tomato & basil soup
Prepare the basic recipe, using 2 cups bouillon and 2 cups soy milk instead of
4 cups bouillon. Serve with a swirl of soy cream in place of pesto or basil.

quick tomato & basil soup
Prepare the basic recipe, but use 1 (28-ounce) can chopped tomatoes, with juice,
instead of fresh tomatoes. Cook in the flavored oil for 5 minutes.

fresh tomato & red pepper soup
Prepare the basic recipe, omitting the basil and adding 2 seeded and sliced red
bell peppers and 1 teaspoon paprika with the bouillon. Purée as instructed or
leave chunky as desired. Serve garnished with basil in place of pesto.

fresh tomato & orange soup
Prepare the basic recipe, omitting the basil and adding the zest and juice of
2 oranges and 1 teaspoon nutmeg with the bouillon. Use cilantro to garnish in
place of basil or pesto.

minted fresh tomato soup
Prepare the basic recipe, using chopped fresh mint in place of the basil. Add
1 tablespoon lemon juice to the finished soup. Use mint to garnish.

variations

silky lentil soup

see base recipe page 56

chunky french lentil soup
Prepare the chunky lentil soup variation above, and use French lentils in place of red lentils, 2 sliced celery stalks in place of the zucchini, and green not red bell pepper. Garnish with parsley.

silken yellow pea soup
Prepare the basic recipe, using 1 cup yellow split peas, soaked overnight in cold water, in place of red lentils. Increase the cooking time to 60 minutes.

mulligatawny soup
Prepare the basic recipe, adding 1 peeled, cored, and chopped green apple with the vegetables. Use 1–2 tablespoons medium curry powder, to taste, in place of the ground cumin, and add 1 teaspoon dried mint. Stir 1 tablespoon lime juice into the blended soup.

lentil soup with baby spinach
Prepare the basic recipe. Stir 1/2 pound baby spinach into the soup when reheating, and cook just until wilted. There is no need to garnish this variation.

leek & potato soup

see base recipe page 59

vichyssoise
Prepare the basic recipe, let cool, then pass through a mesh strainer to ensure the soup is absolutely smooth. Chill in the refrigerator before serving.

creamy potato soup
Prepare the basic recipe, replacing the leeks with 1 large yellow onion. Use soy milk in place of rice or oat milk.

creamy german potato soup
Prepare the creamy potato soup recipe above. When the onion has softened, add 1 1/2 tablespoons celery seeds, 1 tablespoon caraway seeds, and 1 tablespoon cumin seeds, and cook for 1 minute. Blending this soup is optional.

creamy roasted potato & garlic soup
Preheat oven to 400°F. Place 6 unpeeled garlic cloves in a small baking dish and drizzle with olive oil. Bake for 20 minutes, until the outside is lightly browned and the garlic cloves are soft. When cool enough to touch, squeeze each clove to extract the softened garlic. Stir garlic pulp into the soup at the same time as the bouillon. Prepare the creamy potato soup recipe above.

appetizers

Most cuisines have a selection of starters that are
perfect for vegans. This chapter includes recipes to
pass at parties and others that work well at formal
dinner parties. Some of these recipes also make
great light meals, served with a salad and some
good bread.

bissara

see variations page 87

This North African bean dish is very popular in Egypt where it is served with flat bread and fresh vegetable sticks. Fava beans are also known as broad beans.

2 cups large dried fava beans, soaked overnight
   and drained
3 cloves garlic
1/2 cup olive oil
8 cups water
1 small green chile, seeded and chopped

4 tbsp. lemon juice
2 tsp. ground cumin
sea salt and black pepper
paprika
chopped fresh parsley, to garnish

Place the fava beans, garlic, 1/4 cup olive oil, and water in a saucepan. Bring to a boil, cover, then cook over medium heat until the beans are tender, about 1 to 1 1/2 hours, depending on size and freshness of the beans. Drain and cool, reserving 1 1/2 cups of the cooking liquor.

Place the beans and the green chile in a food processor with 1 cup of the reserved liquor. Blend until smooth, adding more of the liquid if necessary to achieve a firm but soft purée. Return the purée to a clean saucepan and stir in the lemon juice, cumin, and salt and pepper to taste. Cook gently for 5 minutes, stirring. Transfer the bissara to a serving bowl. Drizzle with the remaining olive oil, sprinkle with paprika to taste, and garnish with parsley. Serve at room temperature with flat bread and vegetable sticks, if desired.

Serves 6

samosas & fresh mango chutney

see variations page 88

These delicious, spicy Indian starters are easy to make with phyllo pastry. Once you have mastered the first one, constructing the samosas is really easy. For tips on working with phyllo pastry see page 15 [Intro].

4 tbsp. sunflower oil
1 tsp. mustard seeds
2 small onions, finely chopped
2 tsp. curry powder
1/4 tsp. salt
2 potatoes, peeled and finely chopped
1 carrot, peeled and finely chopped
1 cup diced green beans
1 cup frozen peas
1/2 cup water

1 (8-oz.) package phyllo pastry
sunflower oil, for deep-frying

for the chutney
1 ripe mango
1 large shallot, peeled and roughly chopped
2 green chiles, roughly chopped
2 garlic cloves
sea salt

Warm the oil in a skillet, add the mustard seeds, and cook over a moderate heat until they begin to pop. Stir in the onions and fry for 5 minutes until they are soft. Add the curry powder and salt, fry for 1 minute, then add the potatoes, carrot, beans, peas, and water. Cook for 15 minutes on a low heat, stirring occasionally, until the vegetables are tender and the liquid almost evaporated. Remove from the heat and let cool. Cut the phyllo pastry sheets in half to make long strips. Work with one strip at a time, covering the remaining strips with wax paper or a damp cloth to prevent drying out. Place a spoonful of the filling at one end of the strip. Fold over the corner diagonally to form a triangle. Continue the folding to the end of the strip. Seal the ends with a little water. Repeat with the remaining strips.

Serves 4

Two-thirds fill a deep-fryer or wok with sunflower oil and heat to 350°F. Fry the samosas two at a time for 2–3 minutes until golden. Drain on paper towel, then serve hot or at room temperature.

To make the chutney, peel the mango and slice the flesh from the pit, roughly chop, and set aside. In a food processor, process the shallot, chiles, and garlic until smooth. Add the mango and pulse to roughly chop. Season with salt. Transfer to a serving bowl.

spaghettini with pesto

see variations page 89

Pesto comes from Genoa in northern Italy and is made from basil, olive oil, pine nuts, and Parmesan or Pecorino cheese. This vegan version uses nutritional yeast in place of the cheese and tastes just as good. Leftover pesto can be stored in the refrigerator for a few days. Simply spoon it into a jar and cover with a thin layer of olive oil. It is great on potatoes, green beans, or stirred into tomato sauce or soup.

1/3 cup pine nuts	2/3 cup olive oil
2 cups fresh basil leaves, washed and patted dry	sea salt and black pepper
3 cloves garlic	12 oz. spaghettini
1/4 cup nutritional yeast	small black olives (optional)
1 tsp. lemon juice	

First, make the pesto. Place the pine nuts in a skillet over a moderate heat and toast until golden brown, turning continuously to prevent burning. Allow to cool. Place the basil, pine nuts, garlic, and nutritional yeast in a blender, turn on, and gradually add the olive oil in a thin stream until the pesto is the desired consistency. Season to taste with salt and pepper.

Cook the spaghettini in a saucepan of boiling water for approximately 5 minutes, or as stated on the package. Drain and toss with the pesto and garnish with black olives, if desired. Serve immediately.

Serves 4

spinach vadai & coconut chutney

see variations page 90

In India no railway journey would be complete without the smell of freshly cooked vadai at every station. Vadai make great starters and, being high in protein, they are also great for lunch boxes.

1 cup yellow split peas (chana dal)
2 cups shredded fresh spinach, washed
1 small onion, finely chopped
1–1 1/2 green chiles, finely chopped
1 tsp. minced gingerroot
5 curry leaves, finely chopped
1/2 tsp. garam masala or turmeric
2 tbsp. chopped fresh cilantro
sea salt

sunflower oil, to fry

for the coconut chutney
1 cup freshly grated coconut
2 tbsp. chopped onion
1 fresh green chile
2 tbsp. chopped fresh cilantro
1 tbsp. lemon or lime juice
1 tbsp. black mustard seeds

Soak the split peas for at least 2 hours, and then drain. Meanwhile, cook the washed spinach until wilted in a saucepan with no water other than that clinging to the leaves; drain and cool. To make the chutney, combine all the ingredients except the mustard seeds in a blender until coarsely ground, adding a little water if necessary. Heat the mustard seeds in a hot dry pan until they pop. Add to the chutney and adjust the seasoning to taste. Set aside until ready to serve. Put the drained peas in a food processor and blend to a coarse paste without adding any water. Tip into a bowl and stir in the cooked spinach and the remaining ingredients. Using wet hands, form the mixture into small round patties about 1 1/2 inches in diameter. Heat a little sunflower oil in a skillet and fry the vadai in batches, turning to ensure that they are golden brown all over. Drain on paper towels and keep warm until serving.

Serves 4

mushroom herb pâté

see variations page 91

Whether you serve this tasty pâté as an elegant starter or as a sandwich filling, you'll enjoy the pungent earthiness of the mushrooms. Portabella mushrooms are used here for their strong flavor, but there are many mushrooms to choose from. Just pick your favorite.

2 tbsp. olive oil
1 medium onion, chopped
2 garlic cloves, minced
1 lb. portabella mushrooms, sliced
1 sprig fresh rosemary
3/4 cup sunflower seeds

zest of 1 lemon
2 tbsp. nutritional yeast
pinch ground nutmeg
1 tbsp. chopped fresh parsley
1 tbsp. chopped fresh thyme
sea salt and black pepper

Heat the oil in a large saucepan, then add the onion and cook over medium-high heat for 5–7 minutes until soft. Add the minced garlic, mushrooms, and rosemary, and cook until the mushrooms are tender. Continue to cook until most of the liquid from the mushrooms has evaporated; cool. Remove the rosemary.

Put the mushroom mixture in a food processor along with the remaining ingredients. Process until smooth, scraping down the sides once in a while. Shape the pâté into oval quenelles. Heat a dessert spoon in hot water, leave it wet, scoop up some pâté, and roll it between the bowl and the spoon to form a quenelle. Slide it off the spoon and onto a plate. Alternatively, press into ramekins and garnish with fresh herbs. Serve at room temperature with crackers or toast.

Serves 4

melon with ginger & orange syrup

see variations page 92

Ginger is said to be good for digestion, which makes it the perfect ingredient to enjoy at the start of a meal. Make the syrup a day or two ahead of time.

for the syrup
1/4 cup water
1/4 cup fresh orange juice
2 tbsp. chopped and peeled gingerroot
3–4 strips orange zest
1–2 tbsp. agave syrup

for the melon
1 ripe cantaloupe or honeydew melon
4 tbsp. finely chopped crystallized ginger
fresh mint, to garnish

To make the syrup, combine the water, orange juice, ginger, and orange zest in a saucepan, then sweeten to taste with agave syrup. Bring to a boil, then reduce the heat and simmer for 2 minutes. Remove from the heat and let stand 15 minutes, then remove and discard the ginger and orange rind while the syrup is still warm. Cool, then chill for at least 1 hour, or longer if desired.

Arrange the melon on plates in slices or make melon balls and put in bowls. Sprinkle the crystallized ginger on top; chill. Just before serving, drizzle with the syrup and garnish with fresh mint.

Serves 4

cashew spread

see variations page 93

This is the vegan version of a cheese spread. Serve it as a starter with vegetable crudités or crackers, but it is also a great sandwich filler and it works well on baked potatoes. Using raw cashews creates a delicately flavored spread, while toasted cashews produce a fuller flavor.

1 1/4 cups raw or roasted unsalted cashews
juice of 1/2 lemon
1/4 cup water
1 large garlic clove
2 tbsp. nutritional yeast
1 tsp. balsamic vinegar
1/2 tsp. sugar

1/2 tsp. sea salt, or to taste
1/2 tsp. white pepper, or to taste
2 tbsp. toasted sesame seeds
1 tbsp. chopped scallion
1 tbsp. chopped fresh parsley
2 tsp. chopped fresh thyme
fresh herbs and a slice of lemon, to garnish

Soak the cashews for at least an hour in water; drain. Combine the cashews, lemon juice, water, garlic, nutritional yeast, balsamic vinegar, and sugar in a food processor. Process until smooth, scraping down the sides once in a while. Season to taste with salt and white pepper.

Transfer the mixture to a bowl. Stir in the sesame seeds, scallion, and herbs. Serve at room temperature garnished with fresh herbs and lemon.

Serves 4–6

tomato bruschetta

see variations page 94

Here bruschetta is made from big slices of crispy ciabatta, but if you make bruschetta from sliced baguette it becomes perfect finger food. Serve with drinks, especially because it is just as good eaten hot or cold.

4 large, thick slices ciabatta
1 garlic clove, halved
2 tbsp. extra-virgin olive oil
sea salt and black pepper

3 fresh tomatoes, skinned, seeded, and chopped
8 sun-dried tomatoes in oil, roughly chopped
1/2 cup torn fresh basil leaves
oil from jar of sun-dried tomatoes

Preheat the oven to 375°F. Rub each slice of ciabatta with the cut sides of the garlic clove. Arrange the bread on a baking sheet and drizzle with the olive oil. Season with salt and bake for about 10 minutes, turning once, until golden.

Mix the tomatoes, sun-dried tomatoes, and half the basil together. Season to taste with salt and pepper. Spoon on top of the ciabatta slices and arrange on a baking sheet. Drizzle with a little of the oil from the sun-dried tomatoes. Return to the oven for 3 minutes to heat through. Serve garnished with the rest of the basil.

Serves 4

spiced garbanzos

see variations page 95

These tasty little garbanzos are great served with drinks or sprinkled over a salad for added protein. Be warned, they are addictive! They are best eaten the day they are made.

1 1/2 tsp. ground cumin
1 tsp. cayenne pepper
1 tsp. smoked paprika
1/2 tsp. sugar

2 tbsp. olive oil
1 1/2 cups canned garbanzos, drained
1–2 tbsp. tamari

Combine the cumin, cayenne, paprika, and sugar in a bowl and set aside. Put the oil in a skillet over medium heat and cook the garbanzos for about 10 minutes until they are golden brown. Add the spice mixture and toss to combine. Drizzle with the tamari, stirring until evenly coated. Transfer to a plate and cool to room temperature, tossing occasionally to separate.

Makes 1 1/2 cups

tapenade with crudités

see variations page 96

This classic dish is usually flavored with anchovies, so if you are tempted to buy your tapenade, check the ingredients carefully. The vegetables sticks can be prepared a few hours in advance and kept in an airtight container in the refrigerator until needed.

for the tapenade
20 black olives, pitted
2 tbsp. capers
zest and juice of 1 lemon
5 garlic cloves, minced
2/3 cup olive oil
sea salt and black pepper

lemon slices, to garnish
for the vegetable sticks
1 red bell pepper
8 celery stalks
8 baby carrots
1/2 cucumber
8 radishes

To make the tapenade, put the olives, capers, lemon juice and zest, garlic, and oil in a food processor, and blend until smooth. Season to taste with salt and pepper, being careful with the salt because the olives and capers are both already high in salt. Transfer to a serving bowl and garnish with lemon slices.

Cut the pepper into strips. Scrub the carrots with a brush under cold running water to clean. Cut in half lengthwise. Wash the celery and cut into strips. Cut the cucumber into sticks. Wash and trim the radishes. Arrange decoratively on a plate and serve with the tapenade.

Serves 4

hummus with dukkah

see variations page 97

Making your own hummus is a great money saver, and you get to select organic ingredients and adjust the acidity, spices, and texture to suit your tastebuds. You may not need all the dukkah, but keep it in a sealed container and use it on salads or vegetable dishes. Serve this hummus as a dip with toasted pita bread.

for the hummus
1 small onion, chopped
2 tsp. olive oil
4 garlic cloves, minced
1 (15-oz.) can garbanzo beans (or equivalent in home-cooked beans)
1/2 cup tahini
1/4 cup lemon juice
1/4 cup fresh chopped parsley
2 tbsp. chopped jalapeño peppers (optional)

1 tsp. cumin
1/4 tsp. cayenne pepper
1 tsp. salt
for the dukkah
1/4 cup sesame seeds
1/4 cup slivered almonds
2 tbsp. coriander seeds
1 tsp. cumin seeds
sea salt and black pepper

To make the hummus, heat the olive oil in a saucepan, and cook the onions for 5–7 minutes, until soft. Put the onions and all the other ingredients in a food processor, and blend until the hummus reaches your desired texture, adding a little water, if the mixture appears too stiff. To make the dukkah, combine the seeds and almonds in a hot, dry skillet. Toast until golden, then cool. Coarsely grind mixture by pulsing a couple of times in a food processor, or by lightly crushing with a pestle and mortar. Season to taste with the salt and pepper. Sprinkle dukkah over the top of the hummus to serve.

Serves 4–6

bissara

see base recipe page 71

bissara with grilled zucchini

Prepare the basic recipe and spread it onto a platter. Slice 2 zucchini lengthwise
and lay on a cookie sheet. Sprinkle with lemon juice and a little salt and
pepper. Put under a hot broiler until just beginning to char around the
edges. Alternatively, cook the zucchini on a grill. Place the zucchini slices over
the bissara.

pinto bean purée

Prepare the basic recipe, using pinto beans in place of fava beans.

white bean & garlic purée

Prepare the basic recipe, using navy beans in place of fava beans and adding 1 or
2 more garlic cloves.

fresh fava bean bissara

Prepare the basic recipe, using 2 1/2 pounds fresh fava beans in place of the
dried fava beans. To cook, remove the beans from their pods and cook in boiling
water for 10 minutes, until tender; drain and refresh with cold water. Remove the
skins from the beans to reveal the bright green beans inside. Continue as for
basic recipe.

variations

samosas & fresh mango chutney

see base recipe page 72

samosas & minted yogurt
Prepare the basic samosas. In place of the chutney, serve with 1 cup Greek-style yogurt mixed with 1/4 cup chopped fresh mint and 2 teaspoons lime juice. Serve garnished with paprika and fresh mint leaves.

potato, spinach & cashew samosas with fresh mango chutney
Prepare the basic samosas, omitting carrots, beans, and peas. After the potatoes are tender, add 2/3 cup broken cashews and cook for 2 minutes, then add 2 cups chopped fresh spinach and cook until wilted. Stir in 4 tablespoons chopped fresh cilantro. Let cool, then proceed with recipe.

sweet potato & ginger samosas with fresh mango chutney
Prepare the basic samosas, using chopped sweet potato in place of the potato and omitting the carrots and beans. Add 2 teaspoons minced gingerroot and 1 finely chopped green chile with the curry powder.

oven-baked samosas with fresh mango chutney
Prepare the basic recipe, but instead of deep-frying, brush samosas with sunflower oil and put on a parchment-lined cookie sheet. Bake at 400°F for 10–12 minutes.

spaghettini with pesto

see base recipe page 74

arugula pesto
Prepare the basic pesto recipe, replacing the pine nuts with walnuts and the basil leaves with arugula leaves.

cilantro pesto
Prepare the basic pesto recipe, replacing the basil leaves with cilantro leaves.

watercress pesto
Prepare the basic pesto recipe, replacing the pine nuts with walnuts and the basil leaves with watercress leaves.

sun-dried tomato pesto
Sun-dried prepare the basic recipe, then stir in 1/3 cup sun-dried tomatoes, drained and chopped.

spinach vadai & coconut chutney

see base recipe page 75

plain vadai in yogurt sauce
Prepare basic vadai, omitting the spinach. In place of the chutney, make a sauce with 2 cups soy yogurt, 2 tablespoons water, and 1/4 teaspoon each of salt and sugar or to taste. Pour over vadai and garnish with red chili powder, ground cumin, and fresh coriander leaves.

vadai & fresh tomato chutney
Prepare basic vadai. Make a tomato chutney by combining 3 skinned and chopped tomatoes with 1 finely chopped red onion, 1/2 cup freshly chopped mint, 1 tablespoon chile-flavored oil, and 1 teaspoon toasted cumin seeds.

vadai & fresh mango chutney
Prepare basic vadai. Serve with mango chutney (page 72).

red chile vadai & coconut chutney
Prepare the basic recipe, but make a hotter version by using red chiles in place of the green chiles.

mushroom herb pâté

see base recipe page 76

mexican pâté
Prepare the basic recipe, but add 1–2 chopped red chile peppers with the mushrooms and use 1/4 cup chopped fresh cilantro in place of the rosemary, parsley, and thyme. Serve with chunks of avocado dipped in lime juice.

mushroom, herb & walnut pâté
Prepare the basic recipe, but replace the sunflower seeds with 3/4 cup chopped walnuts, which have been soaked in hot water for 2 hours.

mushroom, herb & fennel pâté
Prepare the basic recipe. Toast 2 teaspoons fennel seeds in a dry skillet for a minute or two until they start to pop. Add to the pâté after blending.

mushroom, herb & eggplant pâté
Prepare the basic recipe, using 1/2 pound mushrooms and 1 small eggplant. Cut the eggplant into 1/2-inch-thick slices. Sprinkle with salt and let sit for 1 hour, then wipe off the excess water with paper towel. Roughly chop and cook with the mushrooms.

variations

melon with ginger & orange syrup

see base recipe page 79

gingered melon & strawberry salad with ginger syrup
Prepare the basic syrup, using 1/2 cup water and omitting the orange juice
and zest. Serve the melon along with 1/2 pound fresh, hulled strawberries.

melon & black grape salad with gingered port syrup
Prepare the basic syrup, using 1/4 cup port wine in place of the orange
juice and omitting the zest. Serve the melon along with 1/2 pound black
seedless grapes.

gingered melon salad
Prepare the basic recipe, using a quarter each of a cantaloupe and a
honeydew melon. Add 1/4 pound each green and black seedless grapes and
2 large, sliced plums.

gingered melon & orange soup
Prepare the basic recipe. Blend the melon and the syrup in a food processor
until smooth. Serve in bowls garnished with fresh mint.

cashew spread

see base recipe page 80

cashew coconut spread
Prepare the basic recipe, using full-fat coconut milk in place of water. Add the herbs, if desired.

almond spread
Prepare the basic recipe, using almonds or smoked almonds in place of the cashews and 3 tablespoons olive oil in place of the water. Add the herbs and sesame seeds, if desired.

peppered cashew spread
Prepare the basic recipe, but omit the herbs and sesame seeds. Add 1 (2-ounce) jar pimentos and 1 tablespoon smoked paprika to the food processor with the cashews. For additional bite, add 1–2 tablespoons finely chopped chipotle in adobo sauce.

carrot & raisin cashew spread
Prepare the basic recipe, using 3/4 cup grated carrot and 1/2 cup raisins in place of the scallion, parsley, and thyme.

variations

tomato bruschetta

see base recipe page 81

eggplant bruscetta
One hour before preparing, cut 1 eggplant into 1/2-inch-thick slices, sprinkle with salt, and let sit. Wipe dry with paper towel, brush with olive oil, and season with salt and pepper. Put under the broiler and cook until golden on each side. Meanwhile, prepare the basic bruscetta, but omit the sun-dried tomatoes. Arrange the eggplant on top of the tomato-basil mixture. Broil and finish as in the basic recipe.

tapenade brushetta
Prepare the ciabatta, but omit the tomato topping. Spread with tapenade (page 85) and garnish each piece with 1/4 cherry tomato.

portabella mushroom bruschetta
Prepare the ciabatta, but omit the tomato topping. Cook 1 onion in oil until soft, add 6 ounces sliced mushrooms and 1 teaspoon dried thyme, season with salt and pepper, and cook until the mushrooms are tender. Spread on the ciabatta.

artichoke tomato bruschetta
Prepare the ciabatta. Use 1 (7.5-ounce) jar artichoke hearts, drained and chopped, on top of the tomatoes.

variations

spiced garbanzos

see base recipe page 82

spiced pecans
Prepare the basic recipe, using pecans in place of the garbanzos. Omit oil and dry
roast until golden.

spiced almonds
Prepare the basic recipe, using almonds in place of the garbanzos. Omit oil and
dry roast until golden.

spiced pumpkin seeds
Prepare the basic recipe, using pumpkin seeds in place of the garbanzos. Omit oil
and dry roast until golden.

spiced seed mix
Prepare the basic recipe, replacing the garbanzos with 1/3 cup each of pumpkin
seeds, sunflower seeds, pine nuts, and 2 tablespoons each of sesame seeds and
flax seeds. Omit the oil and dry roast the pumpkin seeds, sunflower seeds, and
pine nuts for 2 minutes. Then add the sesame seeds and flax seeds and continue
to roast until golden before adding the spice mixture and tamari.

variations

tapenade with crudités

see base recipe page 85

mushroom tapenade with crudités
Prepare the basic recipe, using 3 cups sliced mushrooms, cooked in 1/4 cup olive oil. Do not add any more oil to the tapenade.

sun-dried tomato tapenade with crudités
Prepare the basic recipe, using rehydrated sun-dried tomatoes or drained sun-dried tomatoes in oil in place of the olives. Reduce the oil to 1/3 cup and flavor with 2 tablespoons chopped fresh basil.

green olive tapenade with crudités
Prepare the basic recipe, using green olives in place of the black olives.

tapenade-stuffed piquillo peppers
Prepare the basic tapenade, then use it to stuff 1 (7-ounce) can piquillo peppers, drained. Omit the vegetable sticks.

hummus with dukkah

see base recipe page 86

black bean hummus with dukkah
Prepare the basic recipe, using black beans in place of garbanzo beans and cilantro in place of the parsley.

pimento hummus with harissa
Prepare the basic recipe, adding 1/4 cup chopped roasted pimentos (from a jar or freshly cooked). Serve with a small dish of harissa (hot chili sauce from North Africa) in place of the dukkah.

tomato hummus pasta sauce
Prepare the basic recipe. Stir 1 cup hummus into 1 (14-ounce) can crushed tomatoes and heat through without boiling. Serve over penne, garnished, if desired, with dukkah.

hummus pita sandwich with shredded vegetables
Prepare the basic recipe and use the hummus to stuff 4 halved pita breads along with shredded iceberg lettuce, carrot, very finely cut green bell pepper, and alfalfa sprouts. Omit the dukkah.

salads

Preparing salads gives the vegan cook an opportunity to show flair and imagination. The availability of a dazzling array of fresh vegetables, grains, and beans provides endless scope to produce really tantalizing salads that tempt both the eye and the palate.

green salad & ranch-style dressing

see variations page 114

A simple green salad is the perfect accompaniment to most main dishes. This vegan version of the classic American dressing has a wonderful, creamy, tangy bite that shows off the texture and flavors of the salad perfectly. The dressing may be made in advance, as it keeps for up to a week in the refrigerator.

for the ranch dressing
1/2 cup silken tofu
1/4 cup cider vinegar
2 garlic cloves, minced
2 tbsp. olive oil
1 tsp. Dijon mustard
1 tsp. maple syrup
2 tbsp. minced fresh flat-leaf parsley
1/2 tbsp. fresh oregano
1/4 tbsp. fresh thyme

sea salt and white pepper
oat milk, if required
for the salad
1 head Boston or butter lettuce, torn into bite-size pieces
1 small head radicchio, torn into bite-size pieces
1 bunch arugula, tough stems removed
4 scallions, thinly sliced
1 cup alfalfa sprouts

To make the dressing, put all the ingredients except the salt, pepper, and oat milk in a blender. Process until blended. Taste, season with salt and pepper, and add a little oat milk to thin, if needed. Cover and refrigerate.

To make the salad, wash, dry, and prepare the vegetables, and place in a serving bowl.

Just before serving, pour in enough dressing to lightly coat the salad, toss gently, then serve with additional dressing on the side.

Serves 6

tabbouleh

see variations page 115

This is the national dish of Lebanon and each family has its own way of preparing it. This version is heady with the flavor of fresh herbs, but feel free to improvise and stamp your own mark on this flexible dish.

1 cup bulgur wheat
1/4 cup lemon juice
1/4 cup virgin olive oil
1 tbsp. finely chopped white onion
6 scallions, finely chopped
1 (3-oz.) bunch flat-leaf parsley, chopped

1 oz. fresh mint, chopped
sea salt and black pepper
1 head Romaine lettuce
4 ripe tomatoes, quartered
fresh parsley sprigs, to garnish

Put bulgur wheat into a bowl, cover with 2 cups boiling water, and let soak for 20 minutes. Drain, then squeeze to remove water, and transfer into a bowl. Add the lemon juice, oil, onion, scallions, parsley, and mint. Season to taste with salt and pepper. Toss, then chill for at least 1 hour.

To serve, arrange the lettuce leaves around the edge of a platter, spoon the salad in the center, and garnish with the tomatoes and sprigs of parsley.

Serves 4–6

gado gado

see variations page 116

This is an easy version of the Indonesian salad that is characterized by its spicy peanut dressing. For added protein, sliced tempeh can be added.

for the salad
2 medium potatoes
2 carrots, cut into matchsticks
1 cup green beans in 1-inch pieces
1 cup coarsely shredded Chinese cabbage
1 cup bean sprouts
5 leaves Chinese lettuce, horizontally sliced
1/2 cup cucumber in matchstick slices
8 oz. firm tofu, drained and sliced

for the peanut dressing
1 cup crunchy peanut butter
2 cups water
1 small onion, very finely chopped
2 garlic cloves, minced
1 tbsp. brown sugar
1 tsp. rice vinegar
1/2-1 tsp. chili powder
sea salt

Boil the potatoes until just tender, then cut into slices. Parboil the carrots and green beans until tender but still crisp. Blanch the bean sprouts for 10 seconds, drain; repeat with the Chinese cabbage. Layer the vegetables, the Chinese lettuce, and cucumber on individual plates.

In a nonstick skillet, fry the tofu on both sides until golden brown, then drain on a paper towel. Cool and arrange on top of the vegetables.

To make the dressing, combine the peanut butter and water until they are well mixed. Stir in the onion, garlic, brown sugar, and rice vinegar, then add chili powder and salt to taste. Pour the dressing over the vegetables just before serving.

Serves 4

wheat berry salad

see variations page 117

The chewy texture of the wheat berries contrasts beautifully with the soft texture of the fried onions and peppers to make a memorable salad. Serve warm or cold.

1 cup wheat berries
1/2 tsp. salt
3 tbsp. olive oil
1 large yellow onion, sliced
1 small red bell pepper, sliced
1 small green bell pepper, sliced

1 small yellow bell pepper, sliced
3 tbsp. tamari soy sauce
2 tbsp. chopped fresh flat-leaf parsley
black pepper
fresh parsley sprigs, to garnish

Rinse the wheat berries under cold water, then put them in a saucepan with the salt and plenty of water. Bring to a boil, then simmer for 50 minutes, or until tender. Drain and set aside.

Meanwhile, heat the olive oil in a large skillet and cook the onion for about 8 minutes, until golden. Add the sliced peppers and continue to cook until they are soft. Toss the onions and peppers into the wheat berries with the tamari, chopped parsley, and plenty of black pepper. Serve garnished with parsley sprigs.

Serves 6

avocado & tomato salad

see variations page 118

The only fruit that contains more monosaturated fatty acids than the avocado is the olive. Avocados are also extremely high in potassium and are a significant source of vitamins, among which are the B-complex group, especially folic acid — important to those on a meat-free diet. They are also slow-burning and easy to digest. Oh yes, they are also delicious!

2 tbsp. pine nuts
2 avocados, peeled, pitted, and sliced
1 tbsp. lemon juice
3 ripe beefsteak tomatoes, roughly chopped
1 small red onion, finely sliced
8 radishes, trimmed and sliced
2 tbsp. chopped fresh basil

sea salt and black pepper
I head Romaine lettuce, trimmed and roughly torn
for the dressing
3 tbsp. olive oil
1 tbsp. balsamic vinegar
1 small garlic clove, minced

Toast the pine nuts in a dry hot skillet until golden, set aside, and cool. Toss the sliced avocado in lemon juice to prevent it browning, then combine with the tomatoes, onions, and radishes. Season with salt and pepper.

Mix all the ingredients together for the dressing. Pour the dressing over the avocado–tomato mixture. Set aside for at least 30 minutes for the flavors to blend.

Line a salad bowl with the Romaine lettuce, gently add the avocado–tomato mixture, and serve garnished with the pine nuts.

Serves 4

warm potato salad

see variations page 119

Vegans can enjoy a creamy potato salad using either a purchased dairy-free mayonnaise or by making it from scratch. The mayonnaise for this recipe is also delicious in a baked potato, on a sandwich, or with your favorite salad ingredients.

for the mayonnaise
1/2 cup soy milk
4 tbsp. lemon juice
1/2 tsp. Dijon mustard
pinch paprika
approximately 3/4 cup mixed olive oil and
    canola oil
sea salt

for the salad
1 1/2 lbs. small red-skinned potatoes, diced
1 tbsp. chopped fresh dill
1 tbsp. snipped fresh chives
1/2 cup finely chopped red onion
sea salt and black pepper

To make the mayonnaise, place the soy milk, lemon juice, Dijon mustard, and paprika in a bowl. Whisk to combine or use a blender. Slowly add the oil in a thin stream, whisking constantly, until the mayonnaise is thick, then continue with the mixing for 1 minute longer. Chill.

Cook the potatoes in a pan of boiling salted water for 12–15 minutes until just tender. Drain the potatoes and tip into a large bowl. Set aside until just warm. Drizzle the mayonnaise over the potatoes and gently mix. Let stand for at least 15 minutes to allow the potatoes to absorb the flavors. Stir the dill, chives, and red onion into the potatoes, then season to taste with salt and pepper. Serve immediately.

Serves 6

spinach salad

see variations page 120

The contrasting textures and colors of the spinach, garbanzo beans, and tomatoes make this salad look and taste like a feast, while the walnut dressing adds an interesting taste note. It is amazingly good for you too!

1/4 cup pine nuts
4 cups (approx 4 oz.) baby spinach, washed and
    dried
1/4 cup sun-dried tomatoes packed in extra-
    virgin olive oil, chopped
1/4 cup very thinly sliced red onion
1 avocado, peeled, pitted, and sliced
1 (15-oz.) can garbanzo beans

16 cherry tomatoes, halved
1/2 cup whole, pitted black olives
for the walnut vinaigrette
2 tbsp. freshly squeezed lemon juice
1/4 tsp. sugar
1/2 tsp. Dijon mustard
sea salt and black pepper
1/4 cup walnut oil

Toast the pine nuts in a dry hot skillet until golden, set aside, and cool.

Place the spinach in a salad bowl. Carefully toss in the remaining salad ingredients.

To make the vinaigrette, whisk together the lemon juice, sugar, mustard, and salt and pepper to taste in a medium bowl. Continue to whisk while slowly adding the walnut oil in a thin stream, to thicken. Pour the dressing over the salad and toss gently, taking care not to break up the garbanzos and avocado.

Serves 6

lentil & rice-stuffed tomatoes

see variations page 121

Conveniently, brown rice and lentils take the same time to cook, so if you substitute any other rice, cook it separately. If possible, stuff these tomatoes several hours in advance, or even the day before, to allow the flavors time to blend.

1/2 cup green lentils, soaked for at least
   2 hours
1/2 cup brown rice, washed
3 cups vegetable bouillon
8 medium-large ripe tomatoes
1 jalapeño pepper, diced
1 cup diced cucumber
1/2 cup cooked corn

3 scallions, sliced
1/3 cup chopped fresh cilantro or parsley
for the dressing
1/4 cup olive oil
1 tsp. grated lime zest
3 tbsp. fresh lime juice
sea salt and black pepper
1 clove garlic, minced

Drain the soaked lentils and place them in a large saucepan with the brown rice and bouillon. Bring to a boil, reduce the heat, cover, and simmer for 40–45 minutes, until the rice and lentils are cooked. Drain and cool. Meanwhile, cut the tops off the tomatoes. Carefully scoop out the pulp, discarding the seeds but reserving the flesh for stuffing the tomatoes. Invert tomato shells on paper towels to drain. Then make the dressing by whisking together the oil, lime zest and juice, salt, pepper, and minced garlic.

Gently stir the jalapeño, cucumber, corn, scallions, and cilantro or parsley into the cold lentil and rice mixture along with the reserved tomato pulp and the dressing. Scoop the filling into the empty tomato cavities, packing them gently and firmly. Replace the tomato tops. Keep chilled, if making in advance, but serve at room temperature.

Serves 4 or 8

pear & endive salad with caramelized cashews

see variations page 122

Belgian endive has a bright, tangy flavor, which is balanced by the sweetness of the pear and the crispy, caramelized cashews in this salad. If you purchase the endive in advance, store in the refrigerator wrapped in paper, then in a plastic bag because it will turn green and bitter if exposed to light.

for the cashews
1/2 cup cashews
2 tsp. vegetable oil
sea salt
1/4 cup maple or agave syrup

for the salad
4 heads Belgian endive
2 ripe pears, unpeeled

for the dressing
2 tbsp. white wine vinegar
1 tsp. Dijon mustard
1/4 cup olive oil
salt, to taste

Line a plate with parchment paper. Preheat a heavy-bottomed pan over a low-medium heat, then toast the cashews for about 5 minutes, tossing them frequently. Sprinkle the vegetable oil and a little salt over the cashews, and toss to coat. Add the maple or agave syrup, continue to toss for about 30 seconds, until the syrup begins to bubble. Transfer to the parchment paper and allow to cool completely. Break apart. Separate some large leaves of Belgian endive and arrange them around each individual serving plate in a star pattern. Chop the remaining endive and place in the center of the dish. Just before serving, combine all the dressing ingredients in a small bowl. Chop the pears and toss with a little of the salad dressing to prevent the pears from browning, then arrange them over the endive leaves. Sprinkle caramelized cashews over each serving.

Serves 4

spring rain salad

see variations page 123

Harusame noodles or cellophane noodles are commonly used to make delicate salads in Japan. Here they are enlivened with a spicy wasabi and pickled ginger dressing. To give this dish an authentic feel, slice the vegetables as finely as possible.

for the dressing
1 tbsp. white miso
1 tbsp. hot water
1 shallot, minced
1 tbsp. minced pickled ginger
pinch wasabi, to taste
1 tbsp. rice vinegar
1 tbsp. soy sauce
1/2 cup grapeseed oil or canola oil

for the salad
1 3/4 oz. dried harusame noodles, or cellophane noodles (bean thread noodles)
1 small cucumber, cut into very thin strips
1/2 carrot, cut into very thin strips
1 scallion, finely shredded

To make the dressing, mix the miso to a paste with the hot water, and whisk together with the shallot, ginger, wasabi, rice vinegar, and soy sauce. Slowly whisk in the oil in a thin stream, to thicken. Taste and adjust the seasoning, and add more wasabi, if desired.

Bring a saucepan of water to a boil and cook the noodles according to the package directions. Refresh in cold water and drain. Mix the noodles, cucumber, carrot, and scallion in a large salad bowl or in individual serving dishes.

Just before serving, pour the dressing over the salad and toss to mix.

Serves 6

green salad with ranch-style dressing

see base recipe page 99

green salad with grainy mustard dressing
Prepare the dressing, using 1 tablespoon grainy mustard in place of the Dijon. Prepare the salad, adding 1 small cucumber, sliced; 1/2 red bell pepper, sliced; 1/2 yellow bell pepper, sliced; 2 tomatoes, sliced; and 1/2 cup pitted small olives.

green salad with marinated tofu & ranch-style dressing
Prepare the basic recipe, adding 8 ounces prepared marinated or herbed tofu.

green salad with garbanzo beans & ranch-style dressing
Prepare the basic recipe, adding 1 (15-ounce) can garbanzo beans.

green salad with hazelnut dressing
Prepare the salad, but use hazelnut dressing in place of ranch dressing. To make the dressing, whisk together 1/4 cup olive oil, 2 tablespoons cider vinegar, and 2 teaspoons Dijon mustard. Stir in 1/4 cup roasted chopped hazelnuts, then season with sea salt and black pepper.

variations

tabbouleh

see base recipe page 100

couscous tabbouleh
Prepare the basic recipe, using couscous in place of bulgur wheat. In a bowl, mix
1 1/4 cups boiling water and 1/2 teaspoon salt with 1 cup quick-cooking
couscous, cover, and allow to stand for 5 minutes. Fluff with a fork.

quinoa tabbouleh
Prepare the basic recipe, using quinoa in place of bulgur wheat. Boil 2 cups
water and add 1 cup quinoa. Stir, cover, and cook for 12 minutes or until the
germ separates from the seed. Remove from heat and allow to stand for about
3 minutes.

tabbouleh with roasted peppers
Prepare the basic recipe. Put 1 red and 1 green bell pepper, halved and seeded,
under the broiler, and cook until the skin is blackened. Place in a paper bag to
cool, then peel and slice. Arrange on top of the bulgur salad before serving.

tabbouleh with dukkah
Prepare the basic recipe. In a hot, dry pan, toast 1/4 cup each of sesame seeds
and slivered almonds, 1 tablespoon coriander seeds, and 1 teaspoon cumin seeds.
Cool, then, using mortar and pestle, coarsely grind seeds and almonds with the
salt and pepper. Sprinkle over the top of the bulgur salad.

variations

gado gado

see base recipe page 102

indonesian salad with miso sesame dressing
Prepare the vegetables for the basic salad. Instead of the peanut dressing,
combine 1/4 cup miso, 1/3 cup soy sauce, 2 tablespoons sesame oil, 1/4 cup rice
vinegar, and 1/3 cup sesame seeds.

indonesian salad with coconut peanut dressing
Prepare the basic salad and dressing, but when making the dressing, blend 1 cup
of the water in a blender with 1/2 cup flaked coconut or cream of coconut, until
smooth. Then mix with the remaining water and peanut butter before adding
the remaining ingredients. Serve garnished with flaked coconut.

gado gado with peanuts
Prepare the basic recipe, adding 1 cup salted, roasted peanuts with the tofu.

gado gado with rice
Prepare the basic recipe, using 2 cups cooked rice in place of the potatoes.

variations

wheat berry salad

see base recipe page 103

barley salad
Prepare the basic recipe, using barley in place of wheat berries. Dry toast the barley in a heavy-based pan for 3–4 minutes, stirring constantly, then cover with boiling water and simmer for 40 minutes until tender.

wheat berry primavera salad
Prepare the basic recipe, using just 1 bell pepper, and adding 1/2 cup each of blanched sliced carrots, asparagus, and broccoli florets. Use basil in place of parsley.

wheat berry, fruit & nut salad
Prepare the wheat berries and onion for the basic recipe but omit the peppers. In a skillet, toast 1/2 cup chopped walnuts, 1/4 cup pumpkin seeds, and 1/4 cup pine nuts. Toss into the wheat berries and onion along with 1/2 cup raisins and the tamari and pepper.

mixed rice salad
Prepare the basic recipe, using 3 cups cooked mixed rice (a combination of brown, red, and wild rice looks stunning) in place of the wheat berries.

variations

avocado & tomato salad

see base recipe page 104

mexican avocado & tomato salad
Prepare the basic recipe, using cilantro in place of the basil in the salad,
and fresh lime juice in place of the balsamic vinegar in the dressing. Add
1/2 tablespoon finely chopped, pickled jalapeño to the salad.

jeweled avocado & tomato salad
Prepare the basic recipe, using mint in place of the basil in the salad, and
lemon juice in place of the balsamic vinegar in the dressing. Add the seeds
of 1 pomegranate to the salad.

avocado & tomato salad boats
Prepare the basic recipe, omitting the avocados when making the salad.
Halve and pit the avocados without peeling. To serve, pile the salad into the
avocado shells, omit the lettuce, garnish with a lemon wedge, and sprinkle
with paprika.

"mozzarella" avocado & tomato salad
Prepare the basic recipe, adding 8 ounces thinly sliced dairy-free
"mozzarella" cheese alternative to the salad ingredients.

variations

warm potato salad

see base recipe page 107

light potato salad
Prepare the basic recipe, omitting the mayonnaise. Replace with a dressing
made by combining 2 tablespoons olive oil, juice of 1 lemon, 2 teaspoons
wholegrain mustard, and salt and pepper to taste.

red, white & blue potato salad
Prepare the basic recipe, using a combination of mixed colors of small potatoes,
with Peruvian (purple), small red, and small white.

german potato salad
Prepare the light potato salad variation above, adding 1 diced dill pickle with
the dill and chives. Add 8 ounces vegan "hotdog," which has been cooked,
cooled, and sliced.

cold potato salad
Prepare any of the potato salad recipes, but allow the potatoes and
mayonnaise to cool completely before adding the dill and chives. Serve cold.

variations

spinach salad

see base recipe page 108

wilted spinach salad
Prepare the basic recipe, but warm the vinaigrette in a small pan until hot, but not boiling. Pour over the salad and toss to wilt the spinach.

spinach salad with crispy tofu
Prepare the basic recipe. In a large skillet, heat 2 tablespoons oil over medium heat and add 1 block firm tofu, which has been squeezed, drained, and cubed. Cook, turning occasionally, until golden brown. Toss into the salad.

spinach salad with toasted pecans
Prepare the basic recipe, but roast 1/2 cup chopped pecans along with the pine nuts.

spinach salad wrap
Prepare the basic recipe, and use it to fill 4 (10-inch) flour tortillas. Roll up tightly and fold in the ends. Cut tortillas in half and serve, either cold or heated in a microwave for 1 1/2 minutes until warm.

lentil & rice-stuffed tomatoes

see base recipe page 109

lentil & rice-stuffed peppers
Prepare the basic recipe, using 4 red bell peppers in place of the tomatoes. Add the flesh of 1 tomato to the lentil and rice stuffing.

tabbouleh-stuffed tomatoes
Prepare the tomatoes as in the basic recipe, but replace the stuffing with tabbouleh (page 100).

lentil & rice-stuffed tomatoes with garbanzos
Prepare the basic recipe, adding 1 cup canned or cooked garbanzo beans in place of the corn.

lentil & rice-stuffed tomatoes with vegan "cheese"
Prepare the basic recipe, adding to the stuffing 1 cup chopped vegan "cheese" alternative — mozzarella-style, Swiss-style, or Cheddar-style would all work well, depending on availability and your taste preference.

variations

pear & endive salad with caramelized cashews

see base recipe page 110

roasted pear & endive salad with caramelized cashews

Prepare the basic recipe, but core the pears and cut into eighths. Place on parchment paper in an ovenproof dish. Brush or spray with sunflower oil and roast in the oven at 450°F for about 10 minutes, until lightly caramelized. Allow to cool before making the salad.

spinach, pear & endive salad with caramelized cashews

Prepare the basic recipe, using only 3 heads of endive. Do not fan the endive leaves on the plate; instead, line each plate with baby spinach leaves (1 package will be sufficient).

orange & endive salad with caramelized cashews

Prepare the basic recipe, using 2 segmented oranges in place of the pears. Use 1 tablespoon orange juice and 1 tablespoon lemon juice in place of the vinegar in the dressing.

peach & endive salad with caramelized cashews

Prepare the basic recipe, using 2 large ripe, sliced peaches in place of the pears.

variations

spring rain salad

see base recipe page 113

japanese sea vegetable salad
Prepare the basic recipe, using a 2-inch piece dried wakami (or other sea vegetable), hydrated, in place of the scallion. Break 1 sheet toasted nori into smallish pieces and let them fall over the finished salad.

shredded root vegetable salad
Prepare the basic recipe, using 1 carrot, 1/2 daikon root, and 1 Japanese turnip (Hakurei) or regular turnip, all finely sliced, in place of the cucumber. Marinate the root vegetables in the dressing for at least 1 hour before combining with the other ingredients.

japanese sprout salad
Prepare the basic recipe, using only 1 cup of noodles and adding 2 cups bean sprouts. Sprinkle the finished salad with 1 tablespoon toasted sesame seeds.

japanese tofu salad
Prepare the basic salad. Before serving, carefully slice 1 (12-ounce) block silken tofu into small cubes and arrange them around the salad.

vegetable
dishes

Vegetables can be big and bold, have strong or subtle flavors, and come in a range of interesting textures. Mix and match them, experiment with them, and you'll find them to be a far cry from the vegetable dishes that have been dished up so often before.

squash & apricot tagine

see variations page 145

This North African specialty is traditionally made in a conical clay pot called a "tagine," but you can cook it in any pan with a well-fitting lid. Serve with couscous.

1 small zucchini, roughly chopped
1/4 cup olive oil
1 onion, finely chopped
2 cloves garlic, minced
1-inch-piece gingerroot, finely shredded
1/2 tsp. ground cumin
1/2 tsp. ground turmeric
1 tsp. paprika
1/2 tsp. cayenne pepper
1 tsp. ground cinnamon
1 medium-large butternut squash, cut into
    chunks

2 medium potatoes, cut into chunks
2 carrots, thickly sliced
4 oz. green beans, sliced
1 cup roughly chopped dried apricots
1 1/2 cups vegetable bouillon
2 tsp. tomato paste
1 (15-oz.) can garbanzo beans
2 tsp. grated lemon zest
2 tbsp. finely chopped fresh parsley
2 tbsp. finely chopped fresh cilantro
sea salt and black pepper
fresh cilantro, to garnish

Place the zucchini in a pan of boiling water, simmer for 10 minutes, until very soft, drain, and cool. Blend to a smooth purée and set aside. Meanwhile, heat the olive oil in a saucepan, add the onion, and cook over a medium-high heat for 5–7 minutes until soft. Add the garlic and ginger, cook for 1 minute, then add the cumin, turmeric, paprika, cayenne, and cinnamon. Cook for 1 minute. Stir in the squash, potato, carrots, green beans, and apricots until they are coated in the spices. Add the bouillon and tomato paste and bring to a boil. Cover, reduce the heat, and simmer until the squash is tender, about 20 minutes. Add the garbanzo beans, lemon zest, parsley, cilantro, and the zucchini purée. Season to taste with salt and pepper, and serve.

Serves 4

spicy spinach & buckwheat crêpes

see variations page 146

These crêpes are incredibly versatile and can be filled with a wide range of vegetables, dried beans, and nuts. Stuff them with a little leftover stew and you've got a great meal for the family. They are also delicious with sweet fillings such as banana and maple syrup, but add 2 teaspoons of sugar to sweeten the batter. If making crêpes for breakfast, make the batter the night before and keep it in the fridge.

for the crêpes
1 tbsp. egg replacer (page 24)
1/4 cup water
1 1/2 cups nondairy milk
1/4 cup canola oil
1/2 tsp. lemon juice
1/2 tsp. salt
1/2 cup rice flour
1/2 cup buckwheat flour

for the filling
2 lbs. fresh spinach
2 tbsp. canola oil
1 medium onion, finely
    chopped
1 1/2-inch-piece gingerroot,
    grated
1/2 tsp. whole fennel seeds
4 cardamon pods, seeds only,
    crushed

1/4 tsp. chili powder
1/2 tsp. garam masala

for the sauce
1 cup soy yogurt
1/4 cup chopped fresh mint
2 tsp. lime juice

To make the crêpes, whisk together the egg replacer and the water until frothy. Whisk in the other ingredients. Let the batter rest for 30 minutes.

Lightly oil an 8- or 10-inch cast iron or heavy nonstick skillet and place over a medium-high heat. Once hot, pour in about 2 tablespoons of batter. Swirl around so it forms a thin layer on the bottom of the pan. If the mixture does not swirl easily, add a little more nondairy milk to the batter. Cook the crêpe. Once the top is dry and the underside lightly browned, flip and cook the other side for 15–30 seconds — the finished crêpe should be lightly browned

without crispy edges. Stack the crêpes as you make them and keep warm. Cook the spinach in just the water clinging to the leaves until it is just tender; drain, cool, and roughly chop. Heat the oil in a saucepan, then add the onion and cook for 5–7 minutes until soft. Add the gingerroot and spices and cook for 1 minute. Stir in the spinach and turn to coat in the spices. Preheat the oven to 425°F. Put a generous amount of filling down the center of each crêpe, roll it up, then arrange in an oiled baking dish. Bake for 20 minutes. Meanwhile, combine the sauce ingredients and serve with the crêpes. (You can also make and fill the crepes in advance and keep chilled until ready to bake.)

Makes 8–10 crêpes

fennel, bell pepper & tomato tart

see variations page 147

Store-bought puff pastry is a gift to vegan cooks, as most major brands are dairy-free, but check before purchasing. This pie is particularly attractive and is a taste sensation.

1 (15-oz.) can navy beans
2 tbsp. nondairy milk
2 tbsp. vegan pesto (page 74 [Appetizers])
sea salt and pepper
2 heads fresh fennel
1 red bell pepper, seeded and halved

6 tomatoes, peeled and thickly sliced
1/2 tsp. coriander seeds
1/4 tsp. fennel seeds
2 1/2 tbsp. olive oil
1 tsp. lemon juice
1 sheet puff pastry

Preheat oven to 375°F. In a food processor, combine the beans, nondairy milk, and pesto, and process until smooth. Season, and set aside. Trim the base of the fennel, and remove and discard the long green stalks. Cut into 8 wedges and place in a saucepan. Cover with boiling water and simmer for 10 minutes, drain thoroughly, and cool. Meanwhile, put the bell pepper under a hot broiler and cook until the skin blackens, turn and repeat until the whole pepper is charred. Wrap in plastic wrap, let cool, then remove the skin and slice. Carefully unwrap the pastry and lay it on parchment paper on a cookie sheet. (If you can't find pastry sheets, roll out pastry into a rectangle 1/8 inch thick.) With a sharp knife, score a border 1 inch from the edge — this will rise to form the edge of the tart. Spread the bean purée on top of the pastry, taking care to stay within the scored line. Arrange the tomato slices on top, followed by the fennel and pepper. Lightly crush the coriander and fennel seeds and sprinkle over the vegetables with a little salt and pepper. Brush the outside border with olive oil, then drizzle the remaining oil and lemon juice over the vegetables. Bake for about 25 minutes, or until the pastry is risen and golden brown. Slip off the parchment paper and serve warm.
Serves 6

pumpkin & tofu kebabs

see variations page 148

Vegans often feel left out at barbecues. These delicious kebabs provide a tasty solution that will make any vegan feel special. They are easy to prepare, and can be made several hours in advance of the party, wrapped in aluminum foil, and refrigerated until required.

8 baby potatoes
1 (12-oz.) young pumpkin
1 large zucchini
2 red, green, or yellow bell peppers, seeded
2 small red onions
8 cherry tomatoes
12 oz. smoked firm tofu, cut into 1-inch cubes
oil, to brush

for the glaze
1/2 cup olive oil
1 1/2 tbsp. cider or white wine vinegar
2 tbsp. maple syrup
2 tbsp. orange juice
2 tbsp. chopped fresh parsley
1 tbsp. chopped fresh rosemary
2 tbsp. Dijon mustard

Cook the potatoes in a pan of boiling water until almost cooked; drain and pat dry. Meanwhile, whisk together the ingredients for the glaze. Cut the pumpkin, zucchini, and bell pepper into 1-inch pieces. Cut the onions into quarters.

Put the potatoes and vegetables in a shallow dish or container. Pour marinade over vegetables. Cover and refrigerate for at least 1 hour.

Heat the grill to medium-high and brush with a little oil. Alternately thread the vegetables and tofu onto 8 skewers, leaving a little space between each. Put the skewers on the grill and cook, turning frequently and basting with the marinade for about 10 minutes. Remove when the pumpkin and zucchini are tender-crisp.

Serves 4

potato & mushroom phyllo pie

see variations page 149

Phyllo pastry is marvelous—it feels like an indulgent treat, but it is low in fat, looks sophisticated, yet is simple to use. The trick is to work quickly to prevent it from drying out, while keeping unused sheets either covered in wax paper or a damp cloth. (More tips on working with phyllo on page 15.) If you wish, this dish may be prepared in advance, covered in plastic wrap, and kept refrigerated until you're ready to cook it.

1 1/2 lbs. floury potatoes, such as Idaho or
    Yukon Gold, thinly sliced
1 tbsp. olive oil
2 onions, finely sliced
8 oz. cremini mushrooms, sliced
1 tsp. dried dill
1 tbsp. arrowroot
1 cup soy cream
1/4 cup vegetable bouillon

1 tbsp. nutritional yeast
1 bunch scallions, sliced
pinch paprika
pinch ground nutmeg
sea salt and black pepper
6 sheets phyllo pastry
olive oil, to brush
sesame seeds, to sprinkle

Preheat oven to 375°F. Oil an 11x7-inch baking dish. In a large pan of boiling water, blanch the potato slices for 2 minutes, plunge into cold water, drain, and blot off any excess water with a cloth or paper towel. Heat the oil in a skillet, add the onions, and cook over a medium-high heat for 5–7 minutes or until soft. Add the mushrooms and cook until just wilted, then stir in the dill. Mix the arrowroot with 2 tablespoons of the soy cream, then stir in the remaining soy cream, bouillon, and nutritional yeast. In the prepared dish, layer the potatoes, onion-mushroom mixture, and scallions, sprinkling a little of the cream mixture, paprika, nutmeg, salt, and pepper over each potato layer. Pour the remaining cream mixture over the top layer.

Working quickly, cut the phyllo slightly larger than the baking dish. Place the first sheet on top of the vegetables, tuck the overlap down inside the dish, then brush with olive oil. Repeat until all the sheets are used. Brush the top generously with oil and sprinkle with sesame seeds. Score the pastry into portions. Bake for 20–25 minutes, until golden; before serving test that the potatoes are cooked by inserting a knife through the scored pastry.

Serves 4

winter vegetable bake

see variations page 150

Root vegetables make a star appearance in this one-pot wonder.

2 tbsp. olive oil
2 red onions, cut into wedges
1/2 butternut squash, diced
1/2 rutabaga, diced
3 medium carrots, thickly
    sliced
2 medium leeks, trimmed and
    sliced
2 medium parsnips, thickly
    sliced

3 raw beets, quartered
2 celery stalks, sliced
1 tsp. caraway seeds
2 garlic cloves, minced
3 tbsp. tomato paste
1 1/4 cups vegetable bouillon
1 (14-oz.) can crushed
    tomatoes
1 tsp. mixed dried herbs
sea salt and pepper

1 tbsp. cornstarch
1 tbsp. water
for the biscuits
2 cups flour
1 tbsp. baking powder
1/2 tsp. salt
1 tsp. dried rosemary
4 tbsp. soy margarine
3/4 cup soy milk
soy milk, to glaze

Heat the oil in a heavy-duty, ovenproof skillet, then add the onions, squash, rutabagas,
carrots, leeks, parsnips, beet, celery, caraway seeds, and garlic. Cook over a medium-high heat
for 5–7 minutes or until the onions are soft. Add the tomato paste, bouillon, crushed
tomatoes and their juices, and herbs. Season to taste. Bring to a boil, cover, and simmer for
30 minutes. Stir the cornstarch into the water, add a little of the pan juices, then pour the
mixture into the pan, stirring, until the liquid thickens a little. Meanwhile, to make the
biscuits, put all the dry ingredients into a bowl. Blend in the margarine with your fingertips
or a fork, until the mixture resembles fine breadcrumbs. Add the soy milk and stir until a soft,
smooth dough is formed, adding more flour if the dough is sticky. Roll out the dough
3/4 inch thick on a lightly floured surface and stamp out 8 to 9 rounds with a 2-inch cookie
cutter. Preheat oven to 400°F. Arrange biscuits around the edge of the vegetable mixture,
brush the tops with soy milk, and bake for 20–25 minutes, or until risen and golden brown.
Serves 4–6

mediterranean warm roasted vegetable wrap

see variations page 151

These deeply satisfying warm wraps are equally good when served cold. Try them as a lunchbox meal. Simply allow the vegetables to fully cool before constructing the wrap.

1 tbsp. olive oil
1 garlic clove, minced
sea salt and black pepper, to taste
1 red bell pepper, seeded and cut into strips
1 green bell pepper, seeded and cut into strips
1 small yellow squash, seeded and cut into strips

1 small zucchini, cut into strips
1 cup cherry tomatoes
1–2 tsp. balsamic vinegar
1 cup hummus
4 tortillas, warmed
4 oz. baby spinach leaves, washed and dried

Preheat oven to 425°F. In a bowl, combine the oil, garlic, salt, and pepper. Lay all the vegetables in an oiled baking pan, pour in the oil mixture, and toss, taking care to coat each strip. Bake, turning once, until the vegetables are slightly charred and tender, about 40 minutes. Sprinkle with a little balsamic vinegar to taste. Cool slightly; the vegetables should be warm, not hot.

Spread the hummus on the warmed tortillas, lay the raw spinach on the hummus, and top with the roasted vegetables. Roll up the tortillas and tuck in the ends. Serve immediately.

Serves 4

pepperoncini & tofu sandwiches

see variations page 152

This is a great sandwich. It works well with leftover tofu and is good with toasted or untoasted bread. Use roasted bell peppers if pepperoncini are unavailable.

1 tsp. sunflower oil
4 oz. firm tofu, pressed and drained, cut into
    thick slices
1/2 ripe avocado, sliced
1 1/2 tsp. lemon juice
4 tbsp. nondairy mayonnaise

4 slices whole wheat sandwich bread
1 large tomato
3 small pepperoncini peppers, stems removed
    and sliced lengthwise
baby lettuce leaves
sea salt and black pepper

Heat a heavy skillet until very hot. Add the oil, then the tofu slices. Cook over a medium-high heat until golden brown on both sides.

Toss the avocado in 1/2 teaspoon lemon juice. Combine the mayonnaise with the remaining lemon juice. Spread the mayonnaise over the bread, and top with the tofu, avocado, tomato, pepperoncini, and lettuce. Season each sandwich with salt and pepper.

Makes 2 sandwiches

mixed vegetable stir-fry

see variations page 153

How can something so wonderful take so little time to prepare! Just select your noodles with care. Most are fine, but some may contain eggs or butter. Also, watch out for "lactose" on the ingredients list.

8 oz. rice or wheat noodles
1 tbsp. peanut or vegetable oil
1 red chile pepper, sliced
1 garlic clove, sliced
1 lb. mixed fresh vegetables such as bok choy,
    snow peas, baby corn, and broccoli florets

2 tbsp. soy sauce
2 1/2 tbsp. sweet chili sauce
2 cups bean sprouts
2 tsp. sesame oil

Cook the noodles according to package directions; drain.

Meanwhile, heat the oil in a large skillet or wok, and fry the chile and garlic for 1 minute. Add the mixed vegetables and stir-fry over a high heat for 3 minutes. Add the soy sauce and chili sauce, and toss to coat. Add the bean sprouts and continue to stir-fry for 2–3 minutes until the vegetables are tender-crisp. Toss with the noodles and drizzle with the sesame oil; serve immediately.

Serves 4

quick green vegetable curry

see variations page 154

Here's an ideal supper dish suitable for friends or family. Don't feel restricted by the selection of vegetables. Use what is readily available or try using vegetables such as baby eggplants, okra, bok choy, or Chinese broccoli. Serve with a chapati or garlic-flavored naan bread or with rice.

2 tbsp. sunflower oil
1 medium onion, chopped
1 zucchini, sliced
2 tbsp. minced gingerroot
2 garlic cloves, minced
1–2 green chiles, seeded and chopped
2 tsp. ground cumin
1/2 tsp. ground turmeric
1/2 tsp. ground coriander

12 oz. fresh broccoli, cut into florets
1 1/2 cups fresh or frozen green beans
1 cup frozen peas
1 1/2 cups coconut milk
1 cup vegetable bouillon
sea salt
8 oz. fresh baby spinach leaves
1/4 cup chopped fresh cilantro
2/3 cup soy yogurt

Heat the oil in a saucepan, add the onion, and cook over a medium-high heat for 3 minutes. Stir in the zucchini and cook for another 3 minutes, or until the onion is soft. Stir in the gingerroot, garlic, chiles, and spices, and cook for 1 minute.

Add the broccoli, beans, peas, coconut milk, and bouillon. Bring to a boil, reduce the heat, cover, and simmer for about 6 minutes, until the broccoli is just cooked. Season to taste with salt. Stir in the spinach and cilantro. When the spinach is wilted, stir in the yogurt, heat through without boiling, and serve.

Serves 4

antipasto pizza

see variations page 155

This pizza is constructed from the wonderful Italian ingredients that come in jars. There is a huge selection. Try white asparagus, mushrooms, capers, or mixed antipasto. Avoid using commercial pizza sauce — it's way too salty. Prepared pizza bases generally do not contain any prohibited ingredients, but do check the ingredients before purchasing.

1 prepared 12-inch pizza base
1 tbsp. tomato paste
3 tbsp. vegan pesto (page 74)
2/3 cup tomato sauce
black pepper

1/2 cup sun-dried tomatoes in oil, drained
  and sliced
4 artichoke hearts from a jar, quartered
2 roasted red bell peppers from jar, cut into
  1/2-inch strips
12 black olives

Preheat oven to 425°F.

Arrange the pizza base on a sheet pan. Spread with the tomato paste, then with the pesto. Spread with the tomato sauce and season with pepper. Sprinkle evenly all over with the tomatoes, artichoke hearts, bell peppers, and olives.

Bake pizza until the crust browns, about 10 minutes.

Makes 1 pizza

zucchini fritters with tzatziki

see variations page 156

These gluten-free fritters use both spelt and rice flours. If these are unavailable, use whole wheat, all-purpose, or even buckwheat flour – or a combination of flours.

for the tzatziki
1 1/2 cups soy yogurt
1 tbsp. olive oil
1/2 cucumber, shredded
1 clove garlic, crushed or minced
1 tsp. chopped fresh dill or 1/2 tsp. dried dill
sea salt and black pepper
for the fritters
1/2 cup rice flour
1/2 cup spelt flour
1 tsp. baking powder

1/3 cup quick-cooking oats
2 tbsp. nutritional yeast
2 tbsp. chopped fresh mint or 1 tsp. dried mint
1 tsp. ground coriander
2 medium zucchini, coarsely shredded
3 scallions, finely chopped
1 red chile pepper, finely chopped
sea salt and black pepper
1/2 cup soy yogurt
canola oil, to fry

In a small bowl, combine all the ingredients for the tzatziki. Chill until ready to serve. In a bowl, combine the flours, baking powder, oats, yeast, mint, and coriander. Place the zucchini in a clean towel and squeeze out any excess liquid, then add to the flour mixture, tossing to ensure that the pieces are coated in flour. Add the scallions, red chile, and salt and pepper to taste. Gently stir in the yogurt, adding a little water if the mixture feels too dry. Set aside for 10 minutes for the baking powder to begin to activate. Heat a skillet or griddle until very hot, then coat with a little oil. Using about 1/4 cup of fritter batter, drop the batter onto the hot skillet and spread out with a spatula. Cook until bubbles rise to the surface of the fritter and the base is golden brown, then turn and cook the other side. Remove and keep warm while you make the next fritters. Serve with the tzatziki.
Serves 4

malay laksa & tofu puffs

see variations page 157

Deep-fried tofu puffs are popular in Southeast Asia and are good with any Asian-style stew.

1 tbsp. sunflower oil
2 heads bok choy, sliced
2 medium carrots, thinly sliced on diagonal
2 celery stalks, thinly sliced on diagonal
4 oz. baby corn, cut down the center lengthwise
2 garlic cloves, finely sliced
2 (2-inch) pieces gingerroot, shredded
4 cups vegetable bouillon
2 cups canned coconut milk
3 tbsp. tamari
2 tbsp. red curry paste
1–2 tsp. sambel oelek, or another chili paste

1 (1-cup) package miso soup mix
2 stalks lemongrass, smashed
2 sprigs laksa leaves (Vietnamese mint), if
    available, or 1 tsp. dried mint
sea salt
1 (1-lb.) package tofu, pressed, drained, and cut
    into 1-inch pieces
oil for deep frying
4 oz. rice vermicelli noodles
2 cups bean sprouts
1 lime, quartered, to garnish

Heat the oil in a wok or saucepan and stir-fry the bok choy until just wilted, then remove from the pan and set aside. In the same pan, put the carrot, celery, corn, garlic, and ginger. Stir-fry until hot, then add the bouillon, coconut milk, tamari, curry paste, chili sauce, miso soup mix, mint, lemongrass, and laksa sprigs or mint. Season with salt. Simmer for 15 minutes. Remove the lemongrass and laksa stalks. While the stew is cooking, prepare the tofu puffs. Heat oil to 375°F in a wok or deep fryer. Deep-fry the tofu cubes in batches until they are golden brown and puffed. Drain on paper towels and keep warm. Meanwhile, put the noodles in a bowl, cover with boiling water, and let soak for 5 minutes. Drain and divide between 4 warmed bowls. Return the bok choy to the stew pan with the bean sprouts and heat through, pour over the noodles, top with the tofu puffs, and serve with a slice of lime.
Serves 4

squash & apricot tagine

see base recipe page 125

mixed vegetable & apricot tagine
Prepare the basic recipe, using 2 pounds chopped vegetables such as pumpkin, parsnip, sweet potato, and cabbage or kale in place of the squash.

bean & apple tagine
Prepare the basic recipe, using dried apples in place of the apricots and canned fava beans in place of the garbanzo beans.

squash & prune tagine
Prepare the basic recipe, using 1 cup quartered dried prunes in place of the apricots.

squash & apricot tagine with chermoula
Prepare the basic recipe, and serve with a side dish of chermoula. Mix together 1/2 cup lemon juice, 3/4 cup olive oil, 3/4 cup finely chopped fresh cilantro, 1/4 cup finely chopped fresh flat-leaf parsley, 2 minced garlic cloves, pinch each of paprika and cayenne. Season with salt.

variations

spicy spinach & buckwheat crêpes

see base recipe page 126

spicy spinach & garbanzo buckwheat crêpes with minted yogurt
Prepare the basic recipe, adding 1 (15-oz.) can garbanzo beans with
the spinach.

spicy spinach French-style crêpes with minted yogurt
Prepare the basic recipe, using 1 cup all-purpose flour in place of rice
and buckwheat flours. Or, use 1/2 cup each of all-purpose flour and whole
wheat flour.

oven-roasted vegetable crêpes
Prepare the basic recipe, using the roasted vegetables from the
Mediterranean Warm Roasted Vegetable Wrap (page 134) in place of
the spicy spinach. Serve with the minted yogurt sauce, if desired.

creamy mushroom crêpes
Prepare the basic recipe, using the mushroom filling from the
Mushroom Lasagna (page 196) in place of the spinach. Omit the
yogurt sauce.

variations

fennel, bell pepper & tomato tart

see base recipe page 128

roasted asparagus & tomato tart
Prepare the basic recipe, using 1 pound asparagus, trimmed (the thinner
varieties work best) in place of the fennel and bell pepper. Arrange the
asparagus spears in a row, tips in alternate directions, to ensure everyone gets
their share of tips and bases.

leek, tomato & dill tart
Prepare the basic recipe, using 4 leeks, white parts only, in place of the fennel
and peppers. Sweat in a covered pan with 1 tablespoon olive oil and 1 teaspoon
dried dill tips for 5 minutes, then cool before arranging on top of the tomatoes.

mushroom, tomato & thyme tart
Prepare the basic recipe, using 4 large portabello mushrooms, thickly sliced, in
place of the fennel and peppers. Cook in 2 tablespoons olive oil with 1 teaspoon
dried thyme until just wilted and the liquid has evaporated, then cool before
arranging on top of the tomatoes.

roasted vegetable tart
Prepare the basic recipe, using the roasted vegetables from the Mediterranean
Warm Roasted Vegetable Wrap (page 134) in place of the tomatoes, bell pepper,
and fennel.

variations

pumpkin & tofu kebabs

see base recipe page 129

shiitake mushroom kebabs with maple-mustard glaze
Prepare the basic recipe, using 16 shiitake mushrooms in place of the
pumpkin and zucchini. Steam the mushrooms for 2 minutes prior to
preparation to reduce the risk of them splitting and falling off the skewer.

butternut squash kebabs with maple-mustard glaze
Prepare the basic recipe, using butternut squash in place of the pumpkin.
Parboil the butternut squash with the potatoes.

eggplant kebabs with maple-mustard glaze
Prepare the basic recipe, using eggplant in place of the pumpkin. To prepare,
cut a small eggplant into 1-inch cubes and sprinkle with salt. Let sit for
30 minutes, then wipe away the bitter juices with a paper towel.

pumpkin & tofu kebabs with adobo glaze
Prepare the basic kebabs, but in place of the maple mustard glaze combine
1–2 tablespoons chopped canned chipotle chile, 1 tablespoon adobo sauce
(from can), 1/4 cup agave syrup, 1/4 cup freshly squeezed mandarin orange
juice, and 1 tablespoon cider vinegar.

potato & mushroom phyllo pie

see base recipe page 130

potato & mushroom puff pastry pie
Prepare the basic recipe, using puff pastry in place of the phyllo.

potato, pea & tomato phyllo pie
Prepare the basic recipe, but use 1 1/2 cups cooked frozen peas and 2 large peeled, seeded, and chopped tomatoes mixed together in place of the cooked mushrooms.

sweet potato & corn phyllo pie
Prepare the basic recipe, replacing half of the potatoes with sweet potatoes and using 2 cups cooked frozen corn in place of the cooked mushrooms.

caramelized onion & potato phyllo pie
Prepare the basic recipe, omitting the onions, mushrooms and scallions. Instead, cook 1 pound sliced yellow onions in 4 tablespoons olive oil over a very low heat for about 30 minutes, stirring often. Stir in 1 tablespoon sugar, then continue to cook for 10–15 minutes until golden brown. Add the dill and proceed as with the basic recipe.

variations

winter vegetable bake

see base recipe page 133

spicy bean & vegetable bake
Prepare the basic recipe, but omit the beet and add 1 (14-ounce) can navy
or lima beans and 1–2 teaspoons hot chili sauce.

roasted winter vegetable bake
Instead of the basic recipe, place all the vegetables in a roasting pan and
toss with olive oil. Bake in a 425°F oven until just beginning to char on the
edges, about 50 minutes. Put in a skillet and add the tomato paste, bouillon,
crushed tomatoes and juices, and herbs. Season to taste. Bring to a boil, and
simmer, uncovered, for 15 minutes. Continue as with the basic recipe.

apple & pear bake
Instead of the basic recipe, peel, core, and chop 3 pears and 3 Granny Smith
apples, then toss with 3/4 cup sugar and 1 teaspoon apple pie spices. Put in
an ovenproof dish and sprinkle with 3 tablespoons water. Top with the basic
biscuit mixture, adding 2 tablespoons sugar and omitting the rosemary, and
bake as in the basic recipe.

mediterranean warm roasted vegetable wrap

see base recipe page 134

warm roasted eggplant wrap
Prepare the basic recipe, replacing the zucchini and squash with 1 eggplant, which has been cut into strips, salted, allowed to stand, and patted dry.

indonesian wrap
Prepare the basic recipe, using 1 tablespoon soy sauce in place of the balsamic vinegar and spreading the tortillas with peanut dressing (page 102) in place of the hummus.

high-protein mediterranean wrap
Prepare the basic recipe, adding 1/2 soy-based "chicken" cutlet, or sliced smoked or flavored tempeh, to each wrap. Cook the cutlet or tempeh according to the manufacturer's instructions.

"mozzarella" mediterranean wrap
Prepare the basic recipe, adding 4 slices mozzarella-style dairy-free "cheese" to each wrap.

variations

pepperoncini & tofu sandwiches

see base recipe page 136

pepperoncini & tapenade sandwiches
Prepare the basic recipe, omitting the tofu. Spread 1 tablespoon tapenade
(page 85) on each sandwich on top of the avocado slices.

tofu & chile jam sandwiches
Prepare the basic recipe, using 1 tablespoon red chile jam per sandwich in
place of the pepperoncini.

pepperoncini & falafal sandwiches
Prepare the basic recipe, using 2 or 3 falafal balls, sliced in thirds, in place of
the tofu.

tofu & horseradish sandwiches
Prepare the basic recipe, omitting the pepperoncini and adding 1/2 to
1 tablespoon prepared horseradish to the mayonnaise.

variations

mixed vegetable stir-fry

see base recipe page 137

quick mushroom stir-fry
Prepare the basic recipe, replacing the mixed vegetables with 1/2 cup sliced
button mushrooms, 1/2 cup sliced oyster or shiitake mushrooms, 1/2 cup
snow peas, and 1 sliced head bok choy.

quick stir-fry with bamboo shoots & water chestnuts
Prepare the basic recipe, replacing the mixed vegetables with half an
8-ounce can each of bamboo shoots and water chestnuts, 1/2 cup snow
peas, and 1 sliced head bok choy.

mixed vegetable stir-fry with cashews
Prepare the basic recipe, adding 1 cup roasted, unsalted cashews with the
bean sprouts.

mixed vegetable stir-fry with black bean sauce
Prepare the basic recipe, using black bean sauce in place of the sweet
chile sauce.

variations

green vegetable curry

see base recipe page 138

quick vegetable lentil curry
Prepare the basic recipe, adding 1 (15-ounce) can drained lentils with the spinach and yogurt.

thai green vegetable curry
Prepare the basic recipe, using 2 tablespoons Thai curry paste in place of the cumin, turmeric, and coriander.

vegetable curry with marinated tofu
Prepare the basic recipe, adding marinated tofu with the yogurt. To make it, at least an hour before preparation, press, drain, and slice the tofu. Cover with a marinade made from 1 tablespoon each of curry powder, cornstarch, lemon juice, and water. After 1 hour marinating, drain the tofu and discard the marinade. Stir-fry the tofu in oil. Prepare the basic recipe and add the tofu with the yogurt.

antipasto pizza

see base recipe page 141

antipasto pizza with "cheese"
Prepare the basic recipe, top with slices of vegan mozzarella "cheese" and sprinkle with vegan "parmesan" (page 22 or purchased) before baking.

antipasto pizza with smoked tofu
Prepare the basic recipe, top with 1 1/2 cups (4 ounces) shredded smoked tofu.

antipasto ciabatta pizza
Cut 2 ciabatta in half lengthwise to use as the base, then continue as for the basic recipe.

polenta pizza
Make quick-cooking polenta according to the package directions, using 3/4 cup cornmeal. Spread the mixture on 2 oiled and lined 8-inch cake pans and bake until firm, about 12 minutes. Use as pizza bases; continue as for basic recipe.

zucchini fritters with tzatziki

see base recipe page 142

carrot fritters with tzatziki

Prepare the basic recipe, using 2 cups shredded carrots in place of zucchini (there is no need to squeeze the liquid out of the carrots).

corn fritters with tzatziki

Prepare the basic recipe, using 2 cups frozen or canned corn in place of the zucchini (there is no need to squeeze the liquid out of the corn). Use parsley in place of mint.

parsnip fritters with tzatziki

Prepare the basic recipe, replacing zucchini with 2 cups shredded parsnips, which have been blanched in boiling water for 2 minutes, then drained and squeezed dry. Use sage in place of mint.

zucchini fritters with tahini sauce

Prepare the basic fritters, but replace tzatziki with tahini sauce. Combine 1 minced garlic clove, 1/4 cup tahini, 4 tablespoons lemon juice, 1/4 cup soy yogurt, and 1 teaspoon freshly chopped parsley. Season to taste with a little sea salt, a pinch of cayenne pepper, and a few drops of agave syrup.

malay laksa with tofu puffs

see base recipe page 144

sweet & sour assam laksa with tofu puffs
Prepare the basic recipe, but mix a little of the bouillon into 1/4 cup tamarind to create a smooth paste and add to the stew with the remaining bouillon.

laksa with flavored noodles & tofu puffs
Prepare the basic recipe, using flavored rice noodles such as pumpkin and ginger rice noodles, mugwort, or wild yam noodles in place of the vermicelli noodles.

laksa with skiitake, sea vegetables & tofu puffs
Prepare the basic recipe, using 4 ounces shiitake mushroom cut into thick slices in place of the celery. Add 1 piece kombu (kelp) about 4 inches long with the lemongrass; discard it at the same time. Garnish with toasted nori pieces and the tofu puffs.

pumpkin & corn laksa with tofu puffs
Prepare the basic recipe, using 12 ounces pumpkin or butternut squash, cut into chunks, and 4 ounces baby corn, cut in half lengthwise, in place of the bok choy, carrots, and celery.

bean, lentil & nutty dishes

Beans, lentils, and nuts love bold flavors making them perfect in dishes loaded with spices or when combined with rich sauces. They also shine in combination with the zingy flavor of fruit. Some dishes here benefit from slow cooking while others can be rustled up in no time.

refried bean tacos

see variations page 176

Making your own tacos is the one way to be sure that you're getting a truly vegan taco.
The "cheese" here is optional for those who seek authenticity!

1 tbsp. sunflower oil
1 small onion, sliced
1 (14-oz.) can vegetarian refried beans
1 (4-oz.) can chopped green chiles, drained
1/4 cup canned crushed tomatoes
1/4 cup black olives, halved
1 cup nondairy "cheese" (cheddar- or Monterey
    Jack-style)
12 cornmeal taco shells, warmed

for the topping
shredded lettuce
soy yogurt or nondairy sour cream
chopped fresh tomatoes
chopped onion
chopped fresh cilantro

Heat the oil in a skillet, add the onion, and cook over a medium-high heat for 5–7 minutes
or until the onion is soft. Reduce the heat, then stir in the refried beans, green chiles,
tomatoes, and olives. Bring the mixture to a boil, stirring constantly to prevent the beans
from scorching. Stir in the "cheese," if using.

Put the bean mixture into the warmed taco shells and serve with a selection of the toppings.

Serves 4

three bean chili

see variations page 177

Here's comfort food and one that is always a hit with meat-eaters too. Make this recipe in bulk for parties or potluck dinners, or freeze it in meal-size portions. It improves with keeping, so it is a great dish to prepare ahead of time.

2 tbsp. sunflower oil
1 large onion, chopped
3 carrots, chopped
2 green bell peppers, seeded and chopped
3 garlic cloves, minced
2–4 tbsp. chili powder, or to taste
1 tsp. smoked paprika
1 tsp. ground cumin
1 (15-oz.) can kidney beans
1 (15-oz.) can navy beans
1 (15-oz.) can black beans

1 (28-oz.) can crushed tomatoes
1 (4-oz.) can green chiles, chopped and drained
1/2 cup tomato paste
1 cup quartered button mushrooms
2 cups frozen or canned corn
1 tbsp. dried oregano
2 tsp. unsweetened cocoa powder
3 cups vegetable bouillon or beer
1 tsp. sugar
sea salt

Heat the oil in a saucepan, then add the onion and cook for 5–7 minutes until soft. Add the carrots, bell peppers, and minced garlic, and cook for 3 minutes. Add the chili powder, smoked paprika, and cumin, then cook for another minute. Stir in all the remaining ingredients. Bring to a boil, then reduce the heat and simmer for at least 20 minutes. Alternatively, bake at 350°F for 20 minutes. The chili matures with longer cooking.

Serves 6–8

pasta e fagioli

see variations page 178

Some call it a stew, others a soup, but either way this dish makes a wholesome meal. It is a good recipe to cook in bulk for a crowd.

2 tbsp. olive oil
1 medium onion, finely chopped
1 small carrot, finely chopped
1 stalk celery, finely chopped
4 large cloves garlic, chopped
1 cup canned tomato sauce or canned crushed
    tomatoes
1 quart plus 2 cups vegetable bouillon

2 sprigs rosemary, left intact, or 2 tsp. dried
    rosemary
1 large sprig thyme, left intact, or 1 tsp. dried
    thyme
1 large fresh bay leaf or 2 dried bay leaves
1 1/2 cups ditalini or other small pasta
2 (15-oz.) cans cranberry beans
sea salt and black pepper

Heat the oil in a skillet, then add the onion, carrot, and celery. Cook over a medium-high heat for 5–7 minutes or until the onion is soft. Stir in the garlic, tomato sauce or tomatoes, bouillon, and herbs. Bring to a boil. Reduce the heat, cover, and simmer for 30 minutes, stirring occasionally.

Return the stew to a rapid boil and add the pasta and beans. Reduce the heat to medium and cook for 6–8 minutes, until the pasta is just cooked. Remove the herb sprigs, if using, and the bay leaf before serving.

Serves 6

hippie hotpot

see variations page 179

The traditional English Lancashire hotpot consists of lamb, onions, and potatoes layered in a heavy pot and slow-cooked all day. This "hippie" version uses lentils in place of the meat, but is just as fine and filling as its ancestor.

1 cup red lentils, washed
2 1/2 cups vegetable bouillon
2 small carrots, chopped
1 parsnip, chopped
1 bay leaf
1 cup canned tomatoes

1 tsp. dried mixed herbs
1 tbsp. nutritional yeast
sea salt and black pepper
2 medium onions, sliced in circles
1 1/2 lbs. potatoes, sliced
olive oil for brushing

Preheat oven to 325°F. Put the lentils in a saucepan with the bouillon, carrots, parsnip, and bay leaf. Bring to a boil, cover, and simmer for 15–20 minutes until the lentils are soft and the vegetables are cooked. Discard the bay leaf. Stir in the tomatoes, herbs, and nutritional yeast, then season to taste with salt and pepper.

Arrange the lentil mix, onions, and potatoes in layers, sprinkling a little pepper and salt over each potato layer, and finishing with a layer of potatoes. Brush the top generously with oil and bake for about 1 1/2 hours, or until the top is browned and the potatoes are tender.

Serves 4

lentil & quinoa burgers with mango salsa

see variations page 180

These lentil and quinoa burgers have a good texture and go well in a bun or served on their own with the salsa and a green salad. They are quite delicate to handle, but they will firm up if allowed to chill before cooking.

1 cup green or brown lentils
1/2 cup quinoa
1 tbsp. olive oil
1 small onion, finely chopped
1 small carrot, grated
2 tsp. ground cumin
3/4 cup soft breadcrumbs
2 tbsp. chopped fresh parsley
3 tbsp. tomato paste
1 tbsp. soy sauce

1 tbsp. nutritional yeast
2 tbsp. peanut butter
sea salt and black pepper
cornmeal or oats
   for coating
olive oil, for frying
for the mango salsa
1 mango, peeled and chopped
1 medium bell green pepper,
   seeded and chopped

1 small red onion, finely
   chopped
1 jalapeño pepper, finely
   chopped
2 tbsp. lime juice
1 tbsp. pineapple juice or
   orange juice
sea salt and black pepper
chopped fresh cilantro, to
   garnish

Put the lentils and quinoa in a saucepan of boiling water, reduce the heat, and simmer until soft, approximately 20 minutes. Drain and cool, and then use a potato masher to break down the lentils.

To make the salsa, combine all the ingredients in a bowl and set aside.

Meanwhile, heat the oil in a skillet, add the onion, and cook over a medium-high heat for 5–7 minutes or until it is soft. Stir in the carrots and cumin, and cook for 2 minutes.

Combine the lentil-quinoa mixture with the onions and carrots. Stir in the breadcrumbs, parsley, tomato paste, soy sauce, nutritional yeast, and peanut butter. Knead the mixture with your hands until it sticks together. Form the mixture into 8 burgers. Coat each burger in a little cornmeal or oats. Chill, if desired, until ready to cook. To serve, heat 1 tablespoon olive oil in a skillet and fry the burgers over a medium-low heat until crisp and golden on each side, 4–5 minutes. Serve with the mango salsa.

Serves 4

tomato farinata

see variations page 181

It is not a pancake, a frittata, or a tortilla, although it has the qualities of all three. You do have to think ahead to prepare the batter, which needs a couple of hours to rest, but once you start cooking, it is quick and simple to prepare. Try it cold, cut into squares for an unusual picnic treat. Gram flour, also called besan, is made from garbanzo beans. It is available at some large markets, most whole-food stores, and always at Asian grocery stores.

for the farinata
1 cup gram (garbanzo) flour
1 tsp. sea salt
1 cup plus 2 tbsp. warm water
4 tbsp. olive oil
black pepper

for the topping
2 ripe tomatoes, skinned, seeded, and chopped
2 scallions, sliced
4 black olives, quartered
1/2 tsp. red pepper flakes (optional)
1 tbsp. chopped fresh rosemary
1 tsp. lemon juice
sea salt and black pepper

Sift the gram flour into a bowl, add the salt. Pour in the water, stirring constantly, to form a thin smooth batter. Cover with a damp cloth and let rest in a warm place for at least 2 hours. Preheat oven to 425°F. Stir 3 tablespoons of the olive oil into the batter. Put the remaining oil in an 8x8-inch baking pan, then put the pan in the oven briefly until the oil is very hot. Pour in the batter, and arrange the topping ingredients on the surface, sprinkling the surface evenly with each in turn. Bake for about 15 minutes, until golden and crisp. Serve hot or at room temperature.

Serves 4

hungarian nut loaf

see variations page 182

Not the usual heavy nut roast but a lighter-textured loaf that uses lentils as well as nuts.
The tomato-pimento sauce adds moisture and flavor.

1 cup red lentils, rinsed
2 1/2 cups vegetable bouillon
1 bay leaf
1 1/2 tbsp. olive oil
1 large onion, finely chopped
1 leek, white part only, finely
    chopped
1 red bell pepper, seeded and
    chopped
4 oz. cremini or button
    mushrooms, finely chopped
1 cup shredded carrot

1 cup whole Brazil nuts,
    toasted and roughly
    chopped
1 garlic clove, minced
1 tbsp. lemon juice
1 tbsp. tomato paste
1 tbsp. paprika
1 tsp. caraway seeds
    (optional)
3 tbsp. nutritional yeast
2 cups wholemeal
    breadcrumbs

2 tbsp. chopped fresh parsley
sea salt and black pepper
for the tomato-pimento sauce
1 tbsp. tomato paste
1 tsp. paprika
1 (14-oz.) can crushed
    tomatoes
2 canned pimentos, drained
    and chopped
1/4 cup red wine or vegetable
    bouillon
1 tsp. dried sage

Preheat the oven to 375°F. Oil and line a 2-pint loaf pan with parchment paper. Put the
lentils in a saucepan with the bouillon and bay leaf. Bring to a boil, cover, and simmer for
about 15 minutes until the lentils are soft. Discard the bay leaf.

Heat the oil in a saucepan, add the onion, and cook over a medium-high heat for
5–7 minutes or until the onion is soft. Set aside half the onion for the sauce. To the
remaining onion, add the leek, red pepper, mushrooms, and carrot. Cook for 5 minutes
longer. Add all the remaining ingredients. Press the mixture into the prepared pan and bake
for 60 minutes, until a toothpick inserted into the center comes out clean. If the top is

overcooking, cover with aluminum foil halfway though the cooking time. Let cool for 10 minutes before removing from the pan. To make the sauce, put the reserved onion and remaining sauce ingredients, except the parsley, into a pan. Bring to a boil, then reduce the heat, and simmer for 15 minutes. Serve with the loaf.

Serves 6–8

vegetable mole oaxaca

see variations page 183

Every family in Mexico has their own way of preparing this fabulous dish, which originated in Oaxaca, so feel free to experiment with the recipe. Use your favorite chiles, vegetables, and beans, or add raisins or almonds.

1/4 cup toasted pumpkin seeds
1 (14-oz.) can tomatoes
1/4 cup tahini
1 tbsp. sunflower oil
1 white onion, finely chopped
2 cloves garlic, minced
1 green bell pepper, seeded
    and chopped
1 large plantain, sliced

1 small butternut squash,
    chopped
2 medium potatoes
1 jalapeño (for mild) or
    habanero (for spicy) chile
2–4 dried chiles, torn
1 tbsp. paprika
2 tsp. ground cumin
1/4 tsp. ground cloves

1/4 tsp. ground cinnamon
1/2 cup vegetable bouillon
sea salt
1 (15-oz.) can black beans
1 cup frozen corn
1 tsp. sugar
1 1/2 oz. vegan dark chocolate
sliced avocados, lime juice,
    fresh cilantro, to garnish

Preheat oven to 350°F. With the motor of the food processor running, add the pumpkin seeds or almonds and process until very fine. Add the tomatoes and tahini, and blend until smooth. Heat oil in a flameproof casserole, add the onion, and cook over a medium-high heat for 5–7 minutes until soft. Add the minced garlic, bell pepper, plantain, squash, potatoes, and fresh chile. Cook for 3 minutes, before adding the dried chile and the remaining spices. Cook for 1 minute. Add the tomato-tahini mixture and bouillon, and season to taste. Bring to a boil, cover, and cook in the oven for 30 minutes. Remove from the oven and add the beans, corn, and sugar, then stir in the chocolate until melted. Adjust the seasoning and add a little water, if needed; the sauce should be quite thick and rich. Return to the oven for 10 minutes to heat through. Serve generously garnished with avocados dipped in lime juice and with plenty of fresh cilantro.

Serves 4

szechuan-glazed tofu with asparagus & cashew stir-fry

see variations page 184

This upscale stir-fry is sure to impress. Chili garlic sauce is available in the Asian section of large markets or in specialized food stores. If unavailable, use ketchup flavored with garlic powder and Tabasco, to taste.

2 tbsp. peanut or sunflower oil
2 cloves garlic, minced
1-inch-piece gingerroot, grated
1/2 cup sugar
1/2 cup water
2 tbsp. chili garlic sauce
1 tbsp. cider vinegar

1/2 tsp. crushed red pepper flakes
1 (1-lb.) block extra-firm tofu (plain or smoked), pressed, drained, and cut into triangles
1 bunch fresh asparagus, stalks peeled, diagonally sliced

1/2 red bell pepper, diagonally sliced very thinly
4 oz. baby spinach leaves
3/4 cup toasted unsalted cashews
sea salt
chopped scallions, to garnish
steamed rice, to serve

In a small pan, heat 1 tablespoon of the oil, add the garlic and ginger, and cook for 1 minute. Remove from the heat and add sugar, water, chili garlic sauce, vinegar, and red pepper flakes. Return to the heat and bring to a boil, then reduce the heat and simmer for about 15 minutes until the sauce takes on a syrup-like consistency. Set aside and keep warm. Meanwhile, heat the remaining tablespoon of oil in a wok or heavy-based skillet and cook the tofu until golden brown on all sides. Remove the tofu from the pan and keep warm. Stir-fry the asparagus until it is almost tender-crisp, add the red bell pepper and stir-fry for 1 minute, then add the spinach and stir-fry until just wilted. Return the tofu to the pan, add the cashews, and stir to mix. Pour the sweet and spicy sauce over the pan and serve immediately on a bed of rice.
Serves 4

chestnut triangles with cranberry sauce

see variations page 185

This rich chestnut dish is perfect for Thanksgiving. Canned chestnut purée is available in some food stores, but if unavailable, make your own by boiling shelled chestnuts in a little water and soy milk, then blending it to a thick paste.

1 tbsp. sunflower oil
1 large onion, finely chopped
1 garlic clove, minced
4 oz. mushrooms, chopped
1 medium carrot, chopped
1 stalk celery, chopped
1/2 tbsp. soy sauce
1 tbsp. nutritional yeast
1/2 tsp. dried thyme

1/4 tsp. dried sage
1 tbsp. chopped fresh parsley
3/4 cup unsweetened chestnut purée
1/4 cup vegetable bouillon (page 22) or half red wine, half bouillon
1 (12-oz.) package puff pastry sheets, thawed if frozen

2 tbsp. soy milk
black sesame seeds, to sprinkle
for the sauce
1 cup brown sugar
1/2 cup orange juice
8 oz. fresh cranberries
1/2 tsp. ground cinnamon

Heat 1 tablespoon oil in a flameproof casserole, add the onion, and cook over medium-high heat for 5-7 minutes until it is soft. Add the minced garlic, mushrooms, carrots, and celery. Cook for 5 minutes. Add the next seven ingredients, cook for 5 minutes and let cool.

Roll each sheet into 12" square and cut into four 6-inch squares. Put the chestnut mixture in the center of each square. Brush the edges of squares with water, then fold in half to form triangles. Seal edges with a fork, then brush with soy milk and sprinkle with sesame seeds. Place on 2 baking sheets. Cover and let sit in the refrigerator for 1 hour or until required.

Meanwhile, make the sauce. Put the sugar and orange juice into a pan, bring to a boil, then stir in the cranberries and cinnamon. Cook for about 8 minutes until the cranberries are soft but are still holding their shape. Cover and keep chilled until required. Serve at room temperature.

Preheat oven to 400°F. Bake for about 20 minutes, until the pastry is puffed and golden brown. Serve with the cranberry sauce.

Makes 8

refried bean tacos

see base recipe page 159

grilled vegetable & refried bean tacos
Prepare the basic recipe. Cut 2 small zucchini and 2 small yellow squash into 1/4-inch-thick slices, brush with sunflower oil, and sprinkle with lime juice. Grill for 2–3 minutes on each side until cooked and browned. Add to the tacos with the beans.

refried bean & "spicy sausage" tacos
Prepare the basic recipe, adding 1 (12-ounce) package soy chorizo, with its casing removed, to the cooked onion. Fry, stirring frequently, for another 5 minutes before proceeding with the recipe.

refried bean & "ground meat" tacos
Cook 1 (12-ounce) package meatless "ground meat" according to the package directions, then add to the basic recipe.

refried bean burritos
Prepare the basic recipe but spread the bean mixture in a warmed wheat tortilla, roll up, and serve at once.

refried bean dip
Prepare the bean mixture, and serve it with tortilla chips.

three bean chili

see base recipe page 160

three bean chili with cheese & sour cream

Prepare the basic recipe, and serve it garnished with shredded vegan hard cheese substitute such as cheddar or Monterey Jack and some nondairy sour cream or soy yogurt.

three bean chili with tvp

Prepare the basic recipe. Ten minutes before the end of the cooking time, add 1/2 cup TVP (texturized vegetable protein) and up to 1/2 cup water, as needed.

three bean enchiladas

Prepare half of the basic recipe. Warm 2 (10-ounce) cans enchilada sauce. Take 8 medium-size corn or flour tortillas and dip each one in the sauce, fill with the chili, roll up, and put in a baking dish, then cover with the remaining sauce. Bake at 375°F for 20 minutes.

three bean chili potato bake

Prepare half of the basic recipe. Boil 1 pound potatoes, then mash with 2 tablespoons soy margarine and 1/4 cup soy milk; season with salt and pepper. Put the chili in a baking dish and top with the mashed potatoes. Cook at 400°F for 20 minutes or until golden.

variations

pasta e fagioli

see base recipe page 162

slow pasta e fagioli
Soak 1 1/4 cups dried cranberry beans overnight, then drain. Prepare the
basic recipe, adding the beans to the dish with the tomatoes. Cook for about
1 1/2 hours, until the beans are tender.

pasta e lima fagioli
Prepare the basic recipe, using lima beans in place of the cranberry beans.

pasta e fagioli with smoked tofu
Prepare the basic recipe. Stir in 1 (12-ounce) package smoked tofu, crumbled, at
the end of the cooking time.

pasta e fagioli soup
Prepare the basic recipe. Add about 2 extra cups bouillon with the pasta to make
the dish more soupy.

hippie hotpot

see base recipe page 163

green lentil hotpot
Prepare the basic recipe, using green lentils in place of the red lentils, and cooking them for about 30 minutes.

curried lentil hotpot
Prepare the basic recipe, using 1 (10-ounce) jar curry sauce and 1 small chopped apple in place of the tomatoes, herbs, and nutritional yeast.

lentil & sweet potato hotpot
Prepare the basic recipe, using 1 1/2 pounds sliced sweet potatoes in place of the potatoes.

lentil hotpot with "cheesy" topping
Prepare the basic recipe, pouring 1 portion "cheese" sauce (page 23) over the top of the potatoes before baking.

variations

lentil & quinoa burgers with mango salsa

see base recipe page 164

spicy lime, lentil & quinoa burgers with mango salsa
Prepare the basic recipe adding 1–2 finely chopped red chiles and the grated zest and juice of 1 lime to the mixture. If the mixture is too soft, add extra breadcrumbs.

lentil, quinoa & zucchini burgers with mango salsa
Prepare the basic recipe, using grated zucchini in place of the carrot.

lentil & oat burgers with mango salsa
Prepare the basic recipe, omitting the quinoa. Add 1 cup rolled oats with the breadcrumbs.

red lentil walnut burgers with mango salsa
Prepare the basic recipe, using red lentils and omitting the quinoa. Add 1/4 cup rolled oats and 3/4 cup finely chopped toasted walnuts with the breadcrumbs.

tomato farinata

see base recipe page 167

mushroom farinata

Prepare the farinata, omitting the topping. In its place, over medium heat cook 2 medium sliced mushrooms, 1 minced garlic clove, and 1/2 teaspoon cumin in 2 tablespoons olive oil until the mushrooms are tender. Use to top the farinata.

lemon & zucchini farinata

Prepare the farinata, but omit the topping. In its place, over a medium heat, cook 1 sliced small onion in 1 tablespoon olive oil until soft. Add 1 sliced medium zucchini, 2 minced garlic cloves, 1 tablespoon chopped fresh parsley, and the zest and rind of 1 small lemon. Cook until the zucchini is tender, season with salt and pepper. Use to top the farinata.

herbed red onion farinata

Prepare the farinata, omitting the topping. In its place, over a medium heat, cook 1 sliced large red onion in 1 tablespoon olive oil until soft. Add 2 sliced minced garlic cloves and 1 tablespoon each chopped fresh parsley and sage. Cook for 2 minutes, then season with salt and pepper. Use to top the farinata.

variations

hungarian nut loaf

see base recipe page 168

moroccan nut loaf
Prepare the basic loaf recipe, using 2–3 teaspoons harissa in place of the paprika and caraway seeds, and cilantro in place of the parsley. Also use cilantro in place of the sage in the sauce.

indian spiced nut loaf
Prepare the basic recipe, using 1–2 tablespoons curry powder in place of the paprika and caraway seeds in the loaf. Add 1/2 teaspoon each of cumin and chili powder to the sauce, and use 1 tablespoon chopped fresh cilantro in place of the sage.

provençal herbed nut loaf
Prepare the basic recipe, adding 1/4 cup sliced black olives and using herbes du Provence in place of the parsley and caraway seeds in the nut loaf. Use rosemary in place of the sage in the sauce.

mexican spiced nut loaf
Prepare the basic recipe, using 2–3 teaspoons hot chili sauce in place of the paprika and cumin seeds in place of the caraway seeds in the nut loaf. Divide 1 (4-ounce) can chopped green chiles between the nut loaf mixture and the sauce. Omit the pimento in the sauce and season with hot chili sauce, to taste.

vegetable mole oaxaca

see base recipe page 171

seitan & vegetable mole oaxaca
Prepare the basic recipe. While the mole is cooking, fry 12 ounces chopped seitan
in 1 tablespoon oil for 5 minutes, stirring frequently, then add to the mole with
the corn.

tofu & vegetable mole oaxaca
Prepare the basic recipe. Take a 1-pound block of tofu, which has been frozen
and then thawed, and cut it into chunks. Fry the tofu in 1 tablespoon oil until
crispy. Add to the mole with the corn.

vegetable & mango mole oaxaca
Prepare the basic recipe, adding the chopped flesh of 1 mango with the corn.

vegetable mole bake
Prepare the basic recipe. Place a generous portion of the stew in a wheat
tortilla, roll up, and place in an oiled dish. Sprinkle with nondairy cheese and
bake for 20–25 minutes at 375°F until crisp and golden. This is a good way to use
leftover mole.

variations

szechuan-glazed tofu with asparagus & cashew stir-fry

see base recipe page 172

szechuan-glazed tofu with bok choy, broccoli & water chestnut stir-fry
Prepare the basic recipe, using 1 sliced head bok choy and 1 small head broccoli, broken into florets, in place of the asparagus, and sliced water chestnuts in place of the cashews.

szechuan glazed tofu with asparagus & walnut stir-fry
Prepare the basic recipe, using toasted walnut pieces in place of the cashews.

hoisin glazed tofu with asparagus & cashew stir-fry
Prepare the vegetables for the basic recipe. Replace the sauce with a sauce made from mixing 1/3 cup hoisin sauce and 1 tablespoon each of soy sauce, rice wine (or dry sherry), and sesame oil plus 1 teaspoon minced fresh gingerroot.

szechuan black bean, asparagus & cashew stir-fry
Prepare the basic recipe, replacing the tofu with 1 (15-ounce) can black beans, added after the spinach is just cooked.

chestnut triangles with cranberry sauce

see base recipe page 174

chestnut triangles with mushroom-wine gravy
Prepare the chestnut triangles, but replace the cranberry sauce with gravy.
Cook a small onion and 4 ounces sliced mushrooms in 1/4 cup oil until just
soft. Add 1/4 cup flour, cook for 2 minutes, then slowly add 2 cups good
vegetable bouillon, 1/2 cup red wine, 2 tablespoons soy sauce, 1 tablespoon
nutritional yeast, and 1/2 teaspoon each sage and thyme. Cook gently,
stirring constantly, until thickened; season with salt and pepper.

smooth chestnut triangles with cranberry sauce
Prepare the basic recipe, but add the bouillon to the cooking vegetables and
simmer until the carrot and celery are soft. Purée in a blender before mixing
with the chestnut purée and herbs.

black bean & mushroom triangles with cranberry sauce
Prepare the basic recipe, but purée 1 (15-ounce) can black beans and add
with the bouillon in place of the chestnut purée. Add 1/2 teaspoon Tabasco.

chestnut wellington with cranberry sauce
Prepare the basic recipe. Unroll one pastry sheet and place the chestnut
mixture in the center, brush the edges with water and fold the long sides
together, pinch to seal, then seal together both ends. Continue as for basic
recipe cooking for about 40 minutes until golden.

rice, grain &
pasta dishes

In many cultures, vegans and non-vegans alike have

long appreciated the versatility of rice, grains, and

pastas, and their affinity with well-flavored

vegetables. If any of these dishes are new to you,

give them a try and you'll soon be won over.

triple tomato risotto

see variations page 199

This very special risotto combines the rich intensity of roasted cherry tomatoes and flecks of sun-dried tomato with the subtlety of tomato-flavored bouillon.

12 oz. cherry tomatoes, halved
8 garlic cloves, unpeeled
1 tbsp. olive oil
4 cups good vegetable bouillon
1 (15-oz.) can tomato sauce
1 tbsp. oil from sun-dried tomatoes
1 tbsp. soy margarine

4 shallots, finely chopped
2 cups arborio (risotto) rice
1/2 cup white wine
1/4 cup sun-dried tomatoes, finely chopped
1/2 cup chopped fresh basil
sea salt and black pepper

Preheat oven to 400°F. Put the cherry tomatoes and the unpeeled garlic in a single layer in an oiled baking dish and drizzle with the olive oil. Bake for about 30 minutes, until the tomatoes have shrivelled. Cool slightly, then squeeze the flesh out of the garlic, mash with a fork, and set aside. In a small pan, heat the bouillon and the tomato sauce until very hot; keep hot. Heat the tomato oil and margarine in a saucepan on a medium-high heat, then add the shallots and cook for 5–7 minutes until the shallots are soft. Add the rice and stir to coat it with oil, then cook until the grains become translucent, about 1 minute. Add the wine and cook, stirring until absorbed, then add about 1 ladleful of the hot bouillon mixture and continue to cook, stirring frequently, until fully absorbed. Add another ladleful of bouillon and allow it to be absorbed before adding another. Continue this process until the rice is tender, but still firm, and just coated in a thick creamy sauce, about 20 minutes (you may not need all the bouillon). Very gently stir in the roasted cherry tomatoes, mashed garlic, sun-dried tomatoes, and basil, and season with salt and pepper to taste. Serve immediately.

Serves 4

biryani

see variations page 200

Biryani was originally a dish created for the Moghul emperors and was a very complicated affair. This simple variation, which is very easy to cook, is packed with aromatic spices and makes a great party dish.

2 tbsp. sunflower oil
1 large onion, finely sliced
3 garlic cloves, minced
1-inch-piece gingerroot, shredded
2 tsp. black mustard seeds
1 red chile pepper, finely sliced
3 tbsp. madras curry paste
6 oz. each fresh cauliflower, carrot, green beans,
    and potato, cut into chunks

6 oz. whole button mushrooms
4 cups vegetable bouillon
1 cup frozen peas
juice of 2 lemons
large pinch saffron threads
2 cups basmati rice, washed
2 tbsp. chopped fresh cilantro
1 cup unsalted roasted cashew nuts or almonds
1/4 cup golden raisins

Preheat the oven to 350°F. Heat the oil in a flameproof casserole, then add the onion and cook over a medium-high heat for 5–7 minutes until the onion is soft. Add the minced garlic, gingerroot, mustard seeds, and chile. Continue to cook, stirring, until the mustard seeds begin to pop. Stir in the curry paste, add the mixed vegetables and mushrooms, then stir well to coat. Pour in the bouillon, and bring to a boil. Reduce the heat and simmer for 10 minutes, until the vegetables are nearly tender.

Stir in the peas, lemon juice, saffron, and rice, then season to taste with salt. Cover with parchment paper, then with a tightly fitting lid, and bake for 30 minutes, until the rice is tender and the bouillon is absorbed. To serve, sprinkle with cilantro, nuts, and raisins.

Serves 6–8

greek-style stuffed peppers

see variations page 201

To boost the protein level, add a can of kidney beans or some diced firm tofu to the stuffing.

4 large green or red bell peppers
3 tbsp. olive oil
1 medium onion, chopped
2 garlic cloves, crushed
1/2 cup brown rice
2 1/2 cups tomato juice or vegetable juice
1 bay leaf
2 sprigs fresh parsley
2 1/2 tsp. dried oregano

2/3 cup chopped walnuts
1 1/2 tbsp. nutritional yeast
2 tsp. lemon juice
pinch sugar
sea salt and black pepper
2 tbsp. breadcrumbs
1/2 tsp. lemon zest
1 tsp. toasted sesame seeds

Cut a slice off the top of each pepper and remove the center core and seeds. Brush the outside of the peppers with a little of the olive oil, then stand upright in an ovenproof dish. Heat the remaining olive oil in a saucepan, then add the onion and cook over a medium heat for 5–7 minutes until the onion is soft. Add the garlic and cook for another minute. Add the rice, 1 1/4 cups tomato juice, bay leaf, parsley, and 2 teaspoons of the oregano. Bring to a boil, cover, and simmer over low heat, adding a little extra water if the mixture dries out before the rice is cooked, about 40 minutes. Discard the bay leaf and parsley sprigs. Add the walnuts, 1 tablespoon of the nutritional yeast, and lemon juice, then season with the sugar, salt, and pepper. Pile the mixture into the pepper shells. Preheat oven to 350°F. Pour the remaining tomato juice and 1/2 teaspoon oregano around the peppers. Combine the breadcrumbs, remaining 1/2 tablespoon nutritional yeast, lemon zest, and sesame seeds, and sprinkle over the peppers. Bake for 30–40 minutes until the peppers are tender. Serve hot.
Serves 4

caramelized onion polenta pie

see variations page 202

A great dish to cook ahead of time, and it freezes well, too. Hot or cold, it is great accompanied by a salad, particularly one containing lots of ripe, juicy tomatoes.

1 red bell pepper, halved and seeded
1 yellow bell pepper, halved and seeded
1 1/2 tbsp. olive oil
1 1/2 tbsp. soy margarine
3 large yellow onions, finely sliced
3 tbsp. balsamic vinegar
1 tbsp. brown sugar
2 bay leaves
sea salt and black pepper
2 tbsp. chopped fresh parsley

1 tbsp. chopped fresh thyme or 1 tsp. dried thyme
1 cup quick-cooking polenta
for the topping
1/3 cup tomato sauce
2 tbsp. soy cream (optional)
2 tsp. nutritional yeast
1 tsp. paprika
pinch red chili flakes
salt and black pepper

Put the bell peppers under a hot broiler and cook until the skin blackens. Turn and repeat until the whole peppers are charred. Wrap in plastic wrap, allow to cool, then remove the skin and slice. Meanwhile, heat the oil and margarine in a saucepan, add the onions, and cook for 5–7 minutes until soft. Reduce the heat, and stir in the balsamic vinegar, brown sugar, and bay leaves. Continue to cook until the onions are a rich golden brown, about 20 minutes. Remove the bay leaves and season to taste with salt and pepper. Preheat oven to 400°F. Cook the polenta according to the package directions. While hot, stir in the peppers, onions, parsley, and thyme. Check the seasoning. Oil a 9-inch round springform pan or a deep flan dish. Press the polenta mixture into the pan and let cool. Combine the ingredients for the topping, season to taste, and spread over the top of the polenta. To serve, bake at 375°F for 20 minutes until the top has browned.

Serves 6

millet pilaf with tahini-herb sauce

see variations page 203

Nutritionally, millet resembles wheat, providing niacin, vitamin B6, and folic acid along with some calcium, iron, potassium, magnesium, and zinc. If you want fluffy, grainy millet, as for this dish, it is essential to leave it alone while cooking. If you want a soft textured millet, however, keep stirring until it is cooked.

4 tbsp. olive oil
3 garlic cloves
3/4 cup millet
2 medium onions, thinly sliced
4 zucchini, thinly sliced
2 green bell peppers, seeded and thinly sliced
1/2 cup toasted pumpkin seeds
3 tbsp. chopped fresh mint
zest and juice of 1 lemon

sea salt and black pepper
for the tahini-herb sauce
1/2 cup chopped fresh flat-leaf parsley
juice of 2 lemons
1/4 cup water
1/4 cup tahini
1 garlic clove, minced
agave syrup, to taste
sea salt and black pepper

Heat 2 tablespoons of the oil in a pan, add the garlic and millet, and stir to coat all the grains in oil. Cover with plenty of boiling water and simmer for 20 minutes; drain. Meanwhile, heat the remaining oil in a separate pan, and add the onions, zucchini, and bell peppers. Cover and cook over a low heat so the vegetables sweat in their own juices until just soft, stirring occasionally. Make the tahini-herb sauce by combining the ingredients by hand or in a food processor. Adjust the seasoning and sweetness to taste. Set aside. When the millet is cooked, stir in the cooked vegetables, pumpkin seeds, mint, and lemon zest and juice. Season to taste with salt and pepper. Heat through, then serve with the tahini-herb sauce.

Serves 4

yakisoba

see variations page 204

The Japanese equivalent of junk food, this noodle dish is often sold at festivals and as street food, sometimes in a bun, hotdog style. It is quick to make, but to cut down the preparation time further, look for bottled Yakisoba sauce in an Asian food market.

for the sauce
1/3 cup teriyaki sauce
2 tbsp. mirin (rice wine) or apple juice
2 tsp. hot chili sauce
1 lemongrass stalk, soft inner core only, crushed
    and finely sliced
1 tsp. sugar
2 tsp. sesame oil
for the stir-fry
8 oz. soba noodles
1 1/2 tbsp. sunflower oil

1 small onion, sliced
2 garlic cloves, minced
2 carrots, thinly sliced
1/2 head cabbage, shredded
8 oz. firm tofu, pressed, drained, and cut into
    1/2-inch cubes
4 scallions, chopped
1 tbsp. toasted sesame seeds
chopped scallions or shredded seaweed, to
    garnish (optional)
pickled ginger, to garnish (optional)

Combine the sauce ingredients in a small bowl and set aside. Cook the soba noodles in boiling water for about 2 minutes or until they are just cooked. Do not overcook or the noodles become sticky. Drain, rinse in cold water, then drain again. Heat the oil in a large skillet or wok over a medium-high heat. Add the onions, and stir-fry for 2 minutes, then add the garlic, carrots, and cabbage. Stir-fry for 3–5 minutes, until the vegetables are cooked but still firm. Add the tofu, soba noodles, scallions, sesame seeds, and sauce, then cook, tossing to combine, until the noodles and tofu are hot. Serve garnished with chopped scallions or seaweed and strips of pickled ginger, if desired.

Serves 4

sicilian caponata

see variations page 205

This heady dish captures the essence of the Sicilian summer. If strongly flavored fresh tomatoes are available, use them; otherwise, the flavor of canned plum tomatoes is preferable to hard, hothouse ones.

2 large purple eggplants
sea salt
2 tbsp. salted capers
2–3 tbsp. olive oil
1 small red onion, finely chopped
2 stalks celery, chopped
2 garlic cloves, minced
1 tsp. dried oregano
2 tbsp. balsamic vinegar

2 tbsp. chopped fresh flat-leaf parsley
6 fresh tomatoes, skinned and chopped, or
   1 (15-oz. can) chopped tomatoes
8 pitted green olives, halved
black pepper
1 tsp. sugar
8 oz. spaghetti
olive oil, to toss

Cut the eggplant into 1-inch-thick slices, then sprinkle with salt. Leave for 1 hour, then wipe away the bitter juices with a paper towel. Cut into large chunks. Meanwhile, put the capers in water to soak; drain. Heat 2 tablespoons olive oil in a skillet and fry the eggplant slices in batches over a medium-high heat, stirring frequently until they are just golden all over but not cooked through. Add a little more oil, if required, and do not overcook. Stir in the onion, celery, garlic, and oregano. Continue to cook for about 5 minutes, until the onion is soft and transparent. Pour in the vinegar and cook, stirring, until it has evaporated, then add the capers, parsley, tomatoes, and olives. Season to taste with salt, pepper, and sugar; cover, and cook for 15–20 minutes, until the eggplant is tender. Meanwhile, cook the spaghetti following the package directions until *al dente*. Drain, toss with a little olive oil, and serve immediately with the eggplant sauce.

Serves 4

creamy mushroom lasagne

see variations page 206

Supplement white mushrooms with crimini, chanterelle, portabello, oyster, porcini, or shiitake mushrooms to make this lasagne a taste sensation.

8 oz. lasagne noodles
1/2 cup dairy-free "Parmesan"
  (page 22)
2 tbsp. olive oil
1 large red onion, sliced
3 garlic cloves, crushed
1 lb. mixed fresh mushrooms, sliced
2 small leeks, white part only, chopped

2 tsp. dried thyme
1/4 cup dry white wine
1 tbsp. tamari
sea salt and black pepper
béchamel sauce (page 23)
3 tbsp nutritional yeast

For the pasta, cook lasagne according to package instructions. If using a no-cook variety, blanch in boiling water for 2 minutes. Drain and lay out on a kitchen towel or parchment paper. Meanwhile, heat the olive oil in a saucepan, then add the onion and cook over a medium-high heat for 5–7 minutes until the onion is soft. Add the crushed garlic, mushrooms, leeks, and thyme, and cook over a low heat until the mushrooms are tender. Increase the heat, add the wine, allow to bubble for 2 minutes, then remove from the heat. Stir in the tamari and salt and pepper to taste. Make the béchamel sauce, then stir in the nutritional yeast. To assemble the lasagne, pour béchamel sauce (page 23) over the bottom of a dish to form a thin layer, cover with a layer of pasta, coat with one-third of the béchamel sauce, followed by half the mushrooms, sprinkle with a third of the "Parmesan"; repeat, finishing with a generous coating of "Parmesan". Preheat oven to 350°F. Cook for 30 minutes, then increase the heat to 400°F and continue to cook until golden brown, preferably with almost burnt bits around the edges.
Serves 6–8

fusilli with green beans & tomatoes

see variations page 207

The rich tomato base used for this pasta dish is extremely versatile and can be adapted for many uses. If you haven't any red wine on hand, use 2 tablespoons of balsamic vinegar instead and make up the liquid with vegetable bouillon.

2 tbsp. olive oil
1 medium onion, chopped
3 garlic cloves, crushed
1 (2-lb.) can crushed tomatoes
2 tbsp. sun-dried tomato paste
1/2 cup vegetable bouillon
2/3 cup red wine plus 1 tbsp. nutritional yeast

1 lb. fresh green beans
2 tsp. dried Italian herbs
1/2 tsp. sugar
sea salt and black pepper
1 lb. fusilli
olive oil, to coat
fresh basil, to garnish

Heat the oil in a skillet, add the onion, then cook over a medium-high heat for 5–7 minutes or until the onion is soft, then add the crushed garlic. Add the tomatoes, tomato paste, bouillon, wine, green beans, herbs, and sugar. Season with salt and pepper. Bring to a boil, then cook for 20–25 minutes until the green beans are tender.

Cook the fusilli in boiling water for about 10 minutes, or according to the package directions. The pasta should be cooked though but still firm. Drain, toss with olive oil, and serve coated with the sauce and garnished with basil.

Serves 4

variations

triple tomato risotto

see base recipe page 187

oven-baked triple tomato risotto
Prepare the basic recipe, using only 1 1/2 cups tomato sauce and 3 1/2 cups bouillon. After the wine has been absorbed, add all the remaining ingredients, cover, and bake at 350°F for 20 minutes; stir, adding extra bouillon if required, and continue to bake for 10 minutes, or until the rice is tender-firm.

triple tomato risotto cakes
Prepare the basic recipe, then let it cool. Shape the risotto into small cakes and fry in olive oil until golden on both sides. This is an excellent way to use up leftover risotto.

asparagus & tomato risotto
Prepare the basic recipe, using 1 bunch asparagus, chopped and blanched, in place of the cherry tomatoes and garlic.

mushroom & tomato risotto
Prepare the basic recipe, using 1 1/2 cups cooked sliced button mushrooms, in place of the roasted cherry tomatoes and garlic.

variations

biryani

see base recipe page 188

biryani with raita
Prepare the basic recipe, and serve with raita. To 1 cup soy yogurt, add
1/2 cup chopped cucumber, 1/4 cup finely chopped red onion, 1 tablespoon
chopped fresh mint, and salt and lemon juice to taste.

lentil biryani
Prepare the basic recipe, adding 1 cup rinsed brown lentils with the vegetables.

pumpkin biryani
Prepare the basic recipe, using 1 (12-ounce) fresh pumpkin, cut into chunks,
in place of the cauliflower and carrot.

biryani with fresh mango chutney
Prepare the basic recipe and serve with mango chutney (page 72).

greek-style stuffed peppers

see base recipe page 190

stuffed zucchini
Prepare the basic recipe, using 4 large zucchini, with seeds and some pulp scooped out, in place of the bell peppers.

barley-stuffed vegetables
Prepare the basic recipe, using barley in place of rice.

stuffed grape leaves
Prepare the basic recipe, using 1 (8-ounce) jar of grape leaves in place of the peppers and 1/2 cup pine nuts in place of the walnuts. Rinse the leaves in warm water, shake dry, and lay out, vein-side up. Roll 1 tablespoon of the mixture in each leaf. Place the parcels in a baking dish, cover with tomato juice mixture, and weight the stuffed leaves with a plate to prevent unraveling. Omit the crumb topping. Serve cold.

persian stuffed peppers
Prepare the basic recipe, using 2/3 cup cooked lentils (canned or home-cooked) in place of the walnuts, and 1 tablespoon each of fresh parsley and chives in place of the dried oregano. Add 1/2 cup currants to the rice mixture before cooking.

variations

caramelized onion polenta pie

see base recipe page 191

"cheesy" polenta pie
Prepare the basic recipe, using 1 1/2 cups grated nondairy "cheese" in place of the onions.

roasted vegetable polenta pie
Prepare the basic recipe, using the roasted vegetables from the Mediterranean Warm Roasted Vegetable Wrap (page 134) in place of the bell peppers, onions, and herbs.

caramelized onions & tapenade polenta pie
Prepare the basic recipe, but cook without the topping. Spread tapenade (page 85) over the top of the hot pie and return to the oven for 2 minutes, just to heat through. Serve with a dollop of nondairy sour cream or soy yogurt.

mushroom polenta pie
Prepare the basic recipe, omitting the caramelized onions. Instead, cook 1 chopped onion in 2 tablespoons olive oil, add 1 minced garlic clove and 6 ounces sliced mushrooms. Cook gently until the mushrooms are tender. Add 1 tablespoon balsamic vinegar and cook until the liquid has evaporated. Stir into the polenta with the bell peppers and herbs.

millet pilaf with tahini–herb sauce

see base recipe page 193

barley pilaf
Prepare the basic recipe, using barley in place of millet. Dry toast the barley in a heavy-based pan for 3–4 minutes, stirring constantly, then cover with boiling water and simmer for 40 minutes until tender.

rice & almond pilaf
Prepare the basic recipe, using 1 cup long-grain rice in place of the millet. After stirring the rice in the oil and garlic, cook the rice in a vegetable bouillon. Use toasted, slivered almonds in place of the pumpkin seeds.

wild rice pilaf
Prepare the basic recipe, using 1 cup wild rice in place of the millet. After stirring the rice in the oil and garlic, cook the rice in 3 cups vegetable bouillon for about 50 minutes until the grains puff open. Drain and leave covered for 5 minutes.

buckwheat pilaf
Prepare the basic recipe, using 1 cup buckwheat in place of the millet. After stirring the buckwheat in the oil and garlic, cover it with boiling water, and cook for 5 minutes.

variations

yakisoba

see base recipe page 194

kata (crisp fried) yakisoba
Prepare the basic recipe. Once the noodles have boiled, drain thoroughly and pat dry. Alternatively purchase pre-steamed noodles. Heat oil in a deep-fat fryer or deep frying pan to 340°F. Divide noodles into 4 portions, then fry a portion at a time for 6–7 minutes, until they are crunchy. Serve the vegetables and sauce over the noodles.

yakisoba with yellow bean sauce
Prepare the basic recipe, omitting the sauce. Instead, combine 1/3 cup teriyaki sauce; 4 tablespoons yellow bean sauce; 2 teaspoons minced gingerroot; 1 lemongrass stalk soft inner core only, crushed and finely chopped; and 2 teaspoons sesame oil.

yakisoba with "chicken"
Prepare the basic recipe, using soy-based "chicken" in place of the tofu.

yakisoba bun
Prepare the basic recipe and serve in a hotdog bun garnished with vegan mayonnaise and pickled ginger.

variations

sicilian caponata

see base recipe page 195

spicy eggplant pasta
Prepare the basic recipe, adding 1/2–1 teaspoon harissa or Tabasco with
the onions.

sicilian-style squash pasta
Prepare the basic recipe, using 3 cups diced winter squash or 3 large zucchini
in place of the eggplant.

sicilian-style tomato & olive pasta
Prepare the basic recipe, omitting the eggplant. Sauté the onion, celery, garlic,
and oregano in only 1 tablespoon olive oil. Add 2 additional large, fresh
tomatoes, skinned and chopped (or 1 8-ounce can chopped tomatoes), when
making the sauce.

sicilian-style eggplant couscous
Prepare the basic recipe, using couscous in place of spaghetti. In a bowl, mix
1 1/4 cups boiling water and 1/2 teaspoon salt with 1 cup quick-cooking
couscous. Cover and allow to stand for 5 minutes. Fluff with a fork.

variations

creamy mushroom lasagne

see base recipe page 196

vegan lasagne with "cheese"
Prepare the basic recipe, adding 2 cups grated nondairy "cheese" to the béchamel sauce (page 23).

creamy mushroom & fennel lasagne
Prepare the basic recipe, adding 2 sliced fennel bulbs, blanched for 5 minutes, with the mushrooms.

gluten-free mushroom spelt lasagne
Prepare the basic recipe, using spelt lasagne in place of the wheat-based lasagne noodles.

lasagne bolognese
Prepare the basic recipe, using bolognese sauce (page 207) in place of the mushroom filling.

fusilli with green beans & tomatoes

see base recipe page 198

fusilli arrabbiata
Prepare the basic recipe, omitting the green beans. Add to the tomato sauce
1–2 teaspoons crushed red pepper flakes, 1 tablespoon lemon juice, and
1 teaspoon paprika.

spaghetti bolognese
Prepare the basic recipe, using 1/2 pound frozen soy-based "ground meat" in
place of the green beans. Serve with spaghetti in place of fusilli.

spaghetti with pine nuts
Prepare the basic recipe, omitting the green beans. Add 1/2 cup toasted pine
nuts just before serving. Serve with spaghetti in place of fusilli.

fusilli with artichokes
Prepare the basic recipe, omitting the green beans. Add 2 (6-ounce) jars
artichokes and a pinch of red pepper flakes 5 minutes before the end of the
cooking time.

side dishes

Side dishes shouldn't be an afterthought. They are

as integral to the taste and appearance of the meal

as the main dish. Think contrast — select fresh bright

flavors and intriguing textures — and think

artistically about the shape and color of the meal

on the plate.

saffron rice

see variations page 221

Saffron is one of life's luxuries. It adds a lovely flavor to the rice and, with its little speckles of dense color, looks fabulous too. If saffron is outside your budget, use 1 teaspoon of powdered turmeric instead.

3 1/2 cups vegetable bouillon
1/2 tsp. saffron threads, soaked in 1 tbsp.
   hot water
2 bay leaves
1 (2-inch) cinnamon stick

2 whole cloves
1/2 tsp. sea salt
1/2 tsp. dried chili flakes (optional)
2 cups Thai jasmine rice or white basmati rice
1 tsp. lemon juice

Put the bouillon, saffron and soaking water, bay leaves, cinnamon, cloves, salt, and chili flakes, if using, in a saucepan with a tight-fitting lid. Bring to a boil.

If using basmati rice, wash thoroughly to remove excess starch; jasmine rice does not need prewashing. Add the rice to the pan, stir, cover, and simmer over a low heat for 10–15 minutes, until the rice is tender and the liquid is absorbed. Remove from the heat and, keeping the lid in place, let sit for 5 minutes. Discard the bay leaves and cinnamon stick, add the lemon juice, taste, and adjust the seasoning. Fluff with a fork before serving.

Serves 8

appams

see variations page 222

These spongy rice and coconut pancakes are popular in the Christian communities in the southern Indian province of Kerala, where they are served with spicy curries and vegetable stews. However, they are also popular on their own with fresh chutneys or, for a breakfast treat, with coconut and sugar or syrup.

2 tbsp. semolina
2 2/3 cups water
2 cups rice flour
1 tsp. sugar

1 tsp. rapid-rise yeast
1/2 cup full-fat coconut milk
1 tsp. sea salt

Put the semolina and 2 cups water in a pan over a moderate heat. Bring to a boil, stirring continuously, then reduce the heat to low. Continue to cook and stir until a smooth paste is formed; transfer to a bowl and let cool. Add the rice flour, sugar, and yeast. Stir in the coconut milk and remaining water to form a thick batter. Cover with plastic wrap and let rise in a warm place for 3–4 hours, until the batter is bubbly and doubled in volume. Very carefully stir in the salt without beating the air out of the mixture.

Heat an oiled griddle or nonstick skillet over a moderately high heat until very hot, add a ladleful of batter, and spread it out by swirling the pan to form a thin pancake. Cover and cook for 3–4 minutes on one side only so that the base is lightly browned but the top remains very slightly moist; remove from the pan, keep warm, and repeat with the remaining mixture.

Makes 10–12 pancakes

caramelized onion packets

see variations page 223

Cooking food in parchment seals in the flavor. Also, the food steams in its own juices, requiring less fat than pan-cooked vegetables. If you wish to adapt this recipe for the grill, use heavy-duty aluminum foil in place of parchment and cook the packets on a preheated grill for about the same time as the oven-cooked version. These should be served alongside a main dish of choice.

2 tbsp. soy margarine
24 baby onions or shallots, quartered
4 small sprigs fresh thyme
2 tbsp. balsamic vinegar

2 tsp. sugar
sea salt and black pepper
4 (12-inch) square pieces of parchment paper

Preheat oven to 400°F.

Melt the margarine in a pan and add the onions, shaking well to coat the onions evenly in margarine. Put one-quarter of the onions and a sprig of thyme in the center of each of the paper squares, drizzle 1/2 tablespoon balsamic vinegar over each, then sprinkle with sugar, salt, and pepper.

Fold up the squares. It doesn't matter how you do this, but make sure that the seams are well rolled – the packets expand with steam during cooking so they need to be well sealed. Place on a cookie sheet in the oven and cook for 15 minutes, then shake the packets gently to move the contents about slightly, and cook for another 30 minutes, until the onions feel soft if carefully squeezed through a cloth.

Serves 4

wholegrain mustard mash

see variations page 224

The ultimate comfort food is given a tangy twist with the addition of wholegrain mustard.

2 pounds medium Yukon Gold or similar floury
   potatoes
2 garlic cloves
1 cup soy milk
3 cups soy cream

1 bay leaf
sea salt
2 tbsp. olive oil
1 1/2 tbsp. wholegrain mustard
black pepper

Peel the potatoes and cut each into 6 pieces. Peel and lightly crush the garlic. Put potatoes and garlic in a saucepan with the soy milk, cream, bay leaf, and a generous pinch of salt. Cook for about 15–20 minutes, until the potatoes are very tender. Strain, reserving the cooking liquid but discarding the bay leaf and garlic.

Mash the potatoes thoroughly (do not use a blender because the potatoes will become gluey), then fold in enough cooking liquid for the mashed potatoes to become soft and smooth. Stir in the olive oil and the mustard, then season to taste with salt and pepper.

Serves 4–5

rösti

see variations page 225

The aroma of cooking rösti is irresistible! This Swiss potato pancake makes a great accompaniment for almost all dishes that do not contain potato. Rösti is also great on its own as a light lunch treat with a green salad or for breakfast served with grilled tomatoes or baked beans.

2 lbs. potatoes, peeled
1 large yellow onion, very finely chopped
2 tsp. sea salt
1/2 tsp. black pepper

4 1/2 tbsp. olive oil
3 tbsp. chopped fresh chives
2 tbsp. chopped fresh parsley

Bring a saucepan of water to a boil, add the potatoes and parboil for 4 minutes. Immediately remove the potatoes and place in cold water to cool. Once cool enough to handle, roughly shred them into a bowl. Add the onion, salt, pepper, 3 tablespoons of the oil, chives, and parsley.

Heat the remaining oil in a nonstick skillet over a high heat. When it is very hot, add the potato mixture, pressing down firmly with the palm of your hand. Reduce the heat slightly, then cook until golden brown, about 7 minutes. Ease a spatula under the rösti to release, then invert the rösti onto a plate. Slip the rösti back into the pan to cook the second side. If preferred, the second side can be cooked under a preheated broiler.

Serves 4

gingered pumpkin

see variations page 226

The sweetness of the pumpkin is accentuated in this recipe with the addition of maple syrup, which is cut with the sharpness of the ginger.

3 tbsp. olive oil
1 (1-lb.) pumpkin, peeled and cut into 1-inch
   chunks
1 1/2 tsp. minced gingerroot

1 tsp. caraway seeds
1 tbsp. maple syrup
sea salt and black pepper

Heat the oil in a saucepan, then fry the pumpkin and ginger, turning often until the pumpkin is golden brown and crispy on the outside yet soft in the center. Add the caraway seeds and maple syrup, then season with salt and pepper. Toss gently to coat and cook for another 2 minutes.

Serves 4

roasted beets with satsuma–chipotle glaze

see variations page 227

Beets are a feast for the eyes as well as the taste buds. Here they are married with the sweet, tangy flavor of satsumas and balanced by the smoky taste of the pungent chipotle.

5 large fresh beets
1/2 cup fresh satsuma juice
1 tsp. cornstarch
1 tbsp. cider vinegar
1 1/2 tbsp. agave syrup

1 canned chipotle chile, chopped, plus
   1 tsp. adobo sauce
2 tbsp. soy margarine
strips of orange zest, to garnish
chopped fresh flat-leaf parsley, to garnish

Preheat oven to 375°F.

Wash the beets, leaving the roots untrimmed. Put them on a large sheet of aluminum foil and seal into a package. Put the package in a baking pan and roast for about 1 3/4 hours until the beets are tender; let cool. Once the beets are cool enough to handle, slip off the skins, then cut into 1/4-inch slices.

Use 1 tablespoon of the satsuma juice to mix the cornstarch to a paste. Add this paste, vinegar, agave syrup, chile, adobo sauce, and margarine to a saucepan. Cook gently until the sauce has slightly thickened. Add the beet slices and heat through, gently turning the beets to evenly coat with the glaze. Garnish with orange zest and chopped parsley or cilantro.

Serves 6

creamed spinach

see variations page 228

This delicious spinach dish is so quick and easy to make that it will earn its place on your list of favorites. You can make your own nondairy cream cheese and mayo, or purchase them from the health food store. If you are in a hurry, you can leave out the onion and garlic.

1 tbsp. olive oil
1 small onion, finely chopped
1 garlic clove, minced
1 lb. fresh baby spinach, washed
1 cup nondairy cream cheese
1/2 cup nondairy mayonnaise

1/4 cup nutritional yeast
1/4 tsp. garlic granules
1/4 tsp. ground nutmeg
sea salt and black pepper
3 tbsp. toasted slivered almonds, to garnish

Heat the olive oil in a saucepan, add the onion, and cook over a medium-high heat for 5–7 minutes until the onion is soft. Add the minced garlic and cook another minute. Add the spinach and cook with only the water clinging to the washed leaves until just tender; drain and transfer to a warmed serving dish.

Meanwhile, combine the nondairy cream cheese, mayonnaise, nutritional yeast, garlic granules, and nutmeg in a saucepan. Heat gently without boiling, then season with salt and pepper to taste. Pour the sauce over the spinach, toss gently, and garnish with the toasted almonds.

Serves 4

broccoli with tarator sauce

see variations page 229

Versions of tarator sauce are served all over the Middle East, sometimes as a dip, sometimes as a soup, and sometimes, as here, to complement a vegetable or main dish. The common ingredient is always walnuts, although sometimes the sauce is flavored with cucumber, tahini, or even raisins. To make your tarator creamier, add a little soy yogurt.

1 cup whole walnuts
boiling water, to soak
1 large garlic clove, minced
1 3/4 cups soft breadcrumbs
3/4 cup water
1/4 cup olive oil

2 tbsp. lemon juice
1 tbsp. white wine vinegar
pinch ground nutmeg
sea salt and black pepper
1 lb. fresh broccoli, broken into florets

Soak the walnuts in boiling water for 1 hour. Drain and discard the water, then place the walnuts in a food processor with the garlic, breadcrumbs, and about half of the 3/4 cup water. Process until the texture suits your taste; the finer the grind, the smoother the finished sauce. Add the oil, lemon juice, vinegar, and nutmeg, and as much of the remaining water as necessary to make a thick but creamy sauce. Season to taste with salt and pepper. Leave for at least 2 hours to mature, then readjust the salt and vinegar if needed.

Stream the broccoli until tender-crisp. Serve immediately drizzled with some of the warm tarator sauce. Serve the remaining sauce on the side.

Serves 4

variations

saffron rice

see base recipe page 209

lemon rice
Prepare the basic recipe, using 1 teaspoon powdered turmeric in place of the saffron and adding the grated zest and juice of 1/2 lemon. A half cup of cashews and/or 1 teaspoon mustard seeds (cooked for 1 minute in 1 teaspoon oil to pop) may also be added.

coconut rice
Prepare the basic recipe, using 3 ounces creamed coconut to the cooking water in place of the spices.

rice with peas
Prepare the basic recipe, adding 1 cup fresh or frozen cooked peas. This is a good addition for the other variations, too.

vermicelli & rice
Prepare the basic recipe, omitting the saffron. Cook 1 cup vermicelli broken into 1-inch pieces in a skillet with 2 tablespoons sunflower oil until golden. Add to the boiling water with the rice.

variations

appams

see base recipe page 210

appams with onion & chile
Prepare the basic recipe, adding a topping: cook 1 teaspoon black mustard seeds in 1 tablespoon oil until they pop. Add 1 finely chopped medium red onion, cook for 5 minutes. Add 1 sliced green chile and 2 teaspoons cumin seeds, and cook for 2 minutes. Stir in 4 tablespoons chopped fresh cilantro and salt. Cook the appam for 3 minutes, top with a heaping tablespoon of the onion mixture, flip, and cook the second side for 2 minutes.

sweet appams
Prepare the basic recipe, using only a pinch of salt. Just before cooking stir 4 tablespoons sugar into the batter. Cook for 3-5 minutes on one side only. Serve with agave or fruit syrup, shredded fresh coconut, and fruit.

palappam (coconut appams)
Prepare the basic recipe, stirring in an additional 1/4 cup coconut milk (plus 4 tablespoons agave syrup for sweet palappams) to the batter just before cooking. Cook for 3-5 minutes on one side only.

caramelized onion packets

see base recipe page 212

caramelized onion & potato packets
Prepare the basic recipe, with 12 baby onions and 12 small potatoes, scrubbed and quartered.

mushroom packets
Prepare basic recipe, but omit the sugar. Use 1 pound of mushrooms, quartered or sliced if large, in place of the onions. Bake for 15–20 minutes.

onion, bell pepper & peppadew packets
Prepare the basic recipe, but replace 12 of the onions with 1 red bell pepper, cut into 8 pieces; 4 quartered tomatoes; and 8 halved peppadew peppers from a jar. Omit the sugar.

caramelized red onion packets
Prepare the basic recipe, using 8 small red onions, quartered, in place of the baby onions or shallots.

wholegrain mustard mash

see base recipe page 213

creamy mashed potatoes
Prepare the basic recipe, omitting the mustard.

pesto mashed potatoes
Prepare the basic recipe, using 2 tablespoons vegan pesto (page 74) in place of the mustard.

potato & celeriac mash
Prepare the basic recipe, using 1 pound potatoes and 1 pound celeriac, and 1 teaspoon Dijon mustard in place of the wholegrain mustard.

roasted garlic mashed potatoes
Prepare the basic recipe, using the flesh from 6 roasted garlic cloves with the potatoes.

variations

rösti

see base recipe page 215

rösti with onion & caraway
Prepare the basic recipe, adding 1 tablespoon toasted caraway seeds with
the herbs.

rösti with nondairy cheese
Prepare the basic recipe. Add 1 1/2 cups shredded nondairy hard cheese to the
shredded potato mixture.

rösti with leftover vegetables
Prepare the basic recipe. Add 1 cup leftover cooked vegetables, chopped into
small pieces, to the shredded potato mixture.

rösti pizza
Prepare the basic recipe, and just lightly cook the rösti on one side. Spread pizza
sauce over that lightly cooked side and top with slices of mushroom, bell
pepper, and onion. If desired, sprinkle with nondairy "Parmesan" cheese. Place
under a preheated broiler until the vegetables are cooked.

variations

gingered pumpkin

see base recipe page 216

gingered pumpkin with red chile oil
Before cooking the pumpkin and ginger, heat the olive oil over a low heat
with 1 sliced, large red chile; 2 whole unpeeled garlic cloves; 1/4 teaspoon
cumin seeds; and 1 strip of lemon zest. Cook until the garlic is browned,
then strain and proceed as in the basic recipe.

gingered plantain
Prepare the basic recipe, using plantain in place of pumpkin.

gingered rutabaga
Replace the pumpkin with 1 pound roughly chopped rutabaga, parboiled for
5 minutes in boiling water, and drained. Add this to the oil with the ginger
and continue as in the basic recipe.

gingered sweet potato
Replace the pumpkin with 1 pound cubed sweet potato, parboiled for
5 minutes in boiling water, and drained. Add this to the oil with the ginger
and continue as in the basic recipe.

roasted beets with satsuma chipotle glaze

see base recipe page 217

rosemary & orange roasted beets
Prepare the basic recipe, adding 2 sprigs fresh rosemary to the foil packages. Stir 1 teaspoon chopped fresh rosemary into the glaze in place of the chipotle and adobo sauce.

broccoli with satsuma chipotle glaze
Prepare the chipotle glaze. Steam 1 head of broccoli, cut into florets, until tender-crisp. Glaze as with the beets.

chipotle roasted carrot & parsnip
Prepare the basic recipe, roasting 3 parsnips and 3 carrots in place of the beets. Peel and chop the vegetables into 4 pieces, put in an aluminum foil package, drizzle with 1 teaspoon olive oil, and roast for about 1 hour until tender. Slip the carrots and parsnips into the glaze directly from the package.

sweet potato & red onion with satsuma chipotle glaze
Prepare the basic recipe, roasting 1 1/2 pounds sweet potatoes and 2 red onions in place of the beets. Peel and chop the vegetables into 4–6 pieces and continue as in the chipotle variation above.

variations

creamed spinach

see base recipe page 218

creamed kale
Prepare the basic recipe, using 1 pound kale in place of the spinach.

pasta with creamed spinach
Prepare the basic recipe and serve it over 12 ounces cooked pasta such as gnocchi or fusilli.

creamed spinach & leeks
Prepare the basic recipe, adding 3 sliced leeks (white part only) to the pan with the onion. Use just 1/2 pound spinach.

cauliflower "cheese"
Prepare the basic recipe, replacing the spinach with 1 cauliflower, broken into florets and cooked in boiling water until tender. For a more cheesy flavor, add 1 1/2 cups shredded nondairy "hard cheese" to the sauce.

broccoli with tarator sauce

see base recipe page 220

roasted beets with tarator sauce
Prepare the sauce for the basic recipe. Roast the beets (page 217). Spoon the tarator over the hot beets. Also use the beet greens, if you wish; steam them for 5 minutes, or until wilted and just tender.

green beans with tarator sauce
Prepare the basic recipe, using 1 pound green beans in place of the broccoli.

cucumber salad with tarator sauce
Omit the broccoli. Prepare the basic sauce. Make a salad of sliced cucumber sprinkled with a little salt and tossed with 1 tablespoon chopped fresh dill. Lay salad on a bed of watercress and serve with the chilled tarator sauce.

bulgarian tarator soup
Omit the broccoli. Prepare the basic sauce, omitting the vinegar. Stir in 4 cups soy yogurt and 1 finely chopped, peeled cucumber and 1 tablespoon chopped fresh dill. Chill thoroughly before serving.

desserts

There is nothing better than rounding off a meal with a yummy dessert. This selection contains something delectable for everyone — for chocolate lovers, pie or ice cream lovers and for those who like their desserts rich and creamy.

silken chocolate mousse

see variations page 246

This recipe is almost too easy to be true — and non-vegans will be truly astonished when they try this amazing mousse. It is very rich, so serve it in small bowls.

1 (12-oz.) package silken tofu, room
   temperature, drained
10 oz. semisweet vegan chocolate
3 tbsp. maple syrup

1 tsp. vanilla extract
2 tbsp. amaretto or a few drops almond extract
fresh raspberries and mint leaves, to garnish

Beat the tofu by hand or in a food processor until smooth.

In a double boiler, melt the chocolate, stirring frequently until smooth. Add to the tofu with the maple syrup, vanilla, and amaretto or almond extract, and beat by hand to combine.

Pour into small dishes and chill for at least 30 minutes. Serve garnished with raspberries and mint leaves.

Makes 4 large or 6 small servings

pistachio kulfi

see variations page 247

Kulfi is Indian ice cream flavored with pistachio, rosewater, or mango. This version uses coconut and soy milk to replace the traditional slow-cooked sweet milk. It is delicious and lighter than the original. Kulfi molds are conical in shape and can be purchased at some Asian stores; however, silicone muffin pans work really well too.

1/2 cup shelled pistachios
1 tbsp. ground almonds
2 cups soy or almond milk
1 cup full-fat coconut milk
1/2 cup confectioners' sugar

1/2 tsp. crushed cardamom seeds
1 tsp. vanilla extract
few drops almond extract
fresh mango slices or passion fruit pulp,
    to serve

Put the pistachios in a blender and process until chopped. Remove about three-quarters of the pistachios and set aside. Process the remaining pistachios until ground, then add the ground almonds and 1/2 cup of the soy or almond milk. Mix in the remaining ingredients by hand, including the chopped pistachios. If the coconut milk remains a bit lumpy, this is good because it adds to the texture of the kulfi.

Pour the mixture into an ice cream maker and process until the ice cream has set. Pour it into your molds. Alternatively, place the mixture in a freezer container and freeze for about 4 hours, removing from the freezer every hour and mashing with a fork to break down the ice crystals. Transfer into molds to finish freezing. Remove from the refrigerator 10 minutes before serving. Serve with slices of mango or drizzle with passion fruit pulp.

Makes 6

apple strudel

see variations page 248

Using phyllo pastry, this dessert is quick to construct and very impressive when it comes out of the oven. See page 15 for hints on working with phyllo dough.

zest and juice of 1/2 lemon
4 medium Granny Smith apples
1/2 cup finely chopped pecans
1/2 cup soft, fresh breadcrumbs
2 tsp. ground cinnamon

3/4 cup brown sugar
4–6 sheets phyllo pastry (12x17-inch)
1/4 cup canola oil
1/2 cup golden raisins
confectioners' sugar, to finish

Preheat the oven to 350°F. Fill a bowl with cold water and add the lemon juice. Peel and slice the apples, dropping the slices into the water to prevent them from browning. In a separate bowl, combine the pecans, breadcrumbs, cinnamon, and 1/2 cup of the brown sugar. Put the first sheet of phyllo pastry on a clean kitchen towel on your work surface and brush with oil. Sprinkle with a third of the pecan mixture. Put another sheet of phyllo pastry on top, brush with oil, and sprinkle with another third of the pecan mixture; repeat with the third sheet, then lay the fourth sheet on top. Drain the apples and pat dry, then mix them with the remaining sugar, lemon zest, and golden raisins. Lay the apples evenly along the length of the phyllo but no more than halfway across it and leaving a 1/2-inch margin around the edges. Brush the edges with a little water. Roll up the dough lengthwise, like a jelly roll, using the cloth to help support the dough; press your strudel together gently. Place the strudel on a silicone sheet or on parchment paper on a cookie sheet, and bake for about 20 minutes or until golden brown. Serve hot or at room temperature. Serve sprinkled with confectioners' sugar, with a scoop of nondairy ice cream (page 239). If you wish, the strudel may be made ahead of time and reheated for 10 minutes in a hot oven.
Serves 6–8

baked rice pudding

see variations page 249

Comfort food at its best. This version is healthier and lower in fat than the traditional dessert, so it is good for you too. It cooks very slowly in a low oven, so you can bake it while you get on with other things.

5 tbsp. short-grain rice
3 tbsp. brown sugar or 2 tbsp. agave syrup
1 strip lemon zest or 1 vanilla pod
4 1/2 cups soy or other unsweetened
    nondairy milk

1/4 tsp. grated nutmeg
2 tbsp. nondairy margarine or butter

Preheat oven to 300°F. Generously grease a 1-quart ovenproof dish with nondairy butter or margarine. Put the rice, brown sugar or syrup, and lemon zest or vanilla pod in the dish. Gently pour in the milk and stir. Sprinkle the grated nutmeg over the surface of the milk and dot with butter or margarine.

Carefully transfer to the oven and bake for 45 minutes, stir, then let cook for another 75 minutes, by which time a brown crust will have formed and the rice will be fully cooked. Serve hot.

Serves 4

tropical fruit kebabs

see variations page 250

We don't often think about using the barbecue to cook a dessert, but these kebabs make a tasty end to an outdoor meal. If you prepare the kebabs in advance, brush the banana and mango with a little lemon juice to prevent browning, cover with plastic wrap, and keep cool. The syrup can be reheated when required.

for the syrup
1/3 cup nondairy butter
1/3 cup maple syrup
6 cardamom pods, seeds only
1 whole clove
1 (3-inch) cinnamon stick
1/2 tsp. vanilla extract

for the kebabs
1/2 small pineapple
2 ripe mangoes
2 firm bananas
nondairy ice cream (page 239, omitting the chocolate chips) or nondairy yogurt, to serve

In a small pan, melt the nondairy butter and stir in the maple syrup. Crush the cardamom seeds with a mortar and pestle, then add them to the syrup with the clove, cinnamon, and vanilla. Keep warm to infuse while preparing the fruit. Skin and core the pineapple and cut into 1-inch chunks. Cut the mango in half and cut the flesh into large chunks, then remove the skin. Peel the bananas and cut into 1-inch slices. Thread the fruit onto 8 metal skewers, or wooden skewers that have been soaked in water for 30 minutes to prevent burning. Preheat the barbecue coals or the broiler to medium-hot. Remove the clove and cinnamon stick from the syrup. Put the kebabs on an oiled rack and cook, turning once, and basting frequently with the syrup until the fruit is lightly browned on the outside, about 5 minutes. Do not overcook or the fruit will fall apart. Drizzle with any remaining syrup and serve immediately with nondairy ice cream or nondairy yogurt.
Serves 4

chocolate chip soy ice cream with hot chocolate sauce

see variations page 251

A low-fat indulgence, and it's versatile too. For vanilla flavor, simply omit the chocolate.

2 tbsp. arrowroot
1 cup soy milk
2 cups nondairy cream
1/4 cup agave syrup or 1/3 cup sugar
2 tsp. vanilla extract
1 cup small chips of semisweet vegan chocolate

for the chocolate sauce
1/4 cup (1/2 stick) nondairy butter or margarine
3/4 cup brown sugar
2 oz. semisweet vegan chocolate, chopped
3–4 tbsp. soy milk

Mix the arrowroot to a paste with 2 tablespoons of the soy milk; set aside. In a saucepan, combine the remaining milk, nondairy cream, and syrup or sugar, and bring to a boil. While stirring, pour the arrowroot paste into the pan, stirring until the mixture thickens slightly. The mixture will continue to thicken as it cools. Cover the surface with greased parchment paper or plastic wrap to prevent a skin from forming. When the mixture is cool, stir in the vanilla extract and the chocolate chips. Pour the mixture into an ice cream maker and process until the ice cream has set. Alternatively, place in a freezer container and freeze for about 6 hours. Remove from the freezer every 1 1/2 hours and mash with a fork to break down the ice crystals to form a smooth ice cream. To make the sauce, melt the nondairy butter or margarine in a pan, add the sugar, and cook, stirring, over low heat until melted. Add the chocolate and 3 tablespoons soy milk, stir until melted, and add a little more soy milk, if desired. Serve hot over the ice cream.

Makes 1 quart

caramelized apple crisp

see variations page 252

During the fall when the choice of apples at the farmers' market is abundant, this dish comes into its own. Jonagold, Pippin, or Rome are all delicious, and of course, Granny Smith apples are available year-round.

1/4 cup (1/2 stick) soy margarine or
   nondairy butter
3/4 cup brown sugar
5 tart apples, peeled and sliced
3/4 cup whole wheat pastry flour

3/4 cup oat-based muesli
1 tsp. ground cinnamon
1/2 tsp. ground nutmeg
4 tbsp. canola oil
2 tbsp. almond or soy milk

Preheat oven to 400°F. In a skillet, melt the margarine or nondairy butter, then add 1/2 cup of the brown sugar. Cook, stirring constantly, until the sugar has melted. Add the apples and turn to coat in the caramel mixture, then cook for about 10 minutes, stirring frequently, until the apples are cooked but still firm.

Meanwhile, in a bowl, combine the remaining brown sugar with the rest of the ingredients, mixing lightly with the fingertips until the mixture becomes crumbly. Add a little more oil if the mixture is too dry or a little more flour if it is too sticky.

Transfer the apples to a deep pie dish or casserole and top with the crumb mixture. Bake for 30 minutes, or until crisp and golden. Serve with soy vanilla ice cream (page 239, omitting the chocolate chips).

Serves 6

toffeed bananas with coconut cream

see variations page 253

Rich but light, this coconut cream is a wonderful accompaniment to most fruit-based desserts.

for the coconut cream
4 oz. block creamed coconut
1/3 cup coconut milk
1/4 cup soy yogurt

4 firm, ripe bananas
1 tbsp. lemon juice
2 tbsp. brown sugar
pinch ground cinnamon
pinch ground nutmeg
toasted coconut, to garnish

To make the coconut cream, roughly chop the block of creamed coconut into pieces, and put them in a saucepan with the coconut milk. Heat slowly until the coconut has melted, stirring frequently. Remove and let cool. Add the yogurt to the cooled coconut cream, beating until the mixture resembles whipped cream in texture. Let cool and keep refrigerated until required.

Peel the bananas, cut them in half lengthwise, brush with lemon juice, and put in a shallow pan. Sprinkle with the brown sugar and a pinch of cinnamon and nutmeg. Put under a medium-hot broiler until the sugar is beginning to caramelize and the bananas are soft. Serve hot with the coconut cream and garnish with toasted coconut.

Serves 4

no cheesecake with mixed berries

see variations page 254

This creamy dessert is stunning — all the joy of cheesecake with a fraction of the fat.

3 tbsp. soy margarine
8 oz. graham crackers, crushed
1 tbsp. cornstarch
3 tbsp. soy milk
1 (12-oz.) package silken tofu, drained
8 oz. nondairy cream cheese
2/3 cup soy yogurt

juice and zest of 1/2 lemon
egg replacer for 1 egg (page 24)
1 tbsp. water
1/4 cup confectioners' sugar, sifted
1/2 tsp. vanilla extract
1 1/2 cups fresh mixed berries
2 tbsp. mixed fruit jelly, melted

Preheat oven to 350°F. Oil an 8-inch cake pan with a removable base. In a saucepan, melt the margarine. Combine 2 tablespoons of the melted margarine with the crushed graham crackers, then press into the cake pan. Bake for 10 minutes, then set aside.

Meanwhile, to the remaining melted margarine in the saucepan, stir in the cornstarch, then blend in the soy milk. Cook over a low heat until thickened. In a bowl or blender, beat the tofu, nondairy cream cheese, yogurt, and lemon juice and zest until smooth. In a cup, whisk the egg replacer with the water (or as directed on the package) until frothy, and stir into the tofu mixture. Mix in the cornstarch mixture, confectioners' sugar, and vanilla. Pour the mixture over the prepared base and cook for 30 minutes, or until the edge of the cheesecake just begins to color. The center will still feel wobbly, but it will firm up when cool. When the cheesecake is cool, arrange the berries on top and lightly brush them with the melted jelly to glaze. Place the cheesecake in the refrigerator to chill. Serve straight from the refrigerator.

Serves 8–10

strawberry tart

see variations page 255

Simple and easy to prepare, a seasonal fruit tart looks and tastes wonderful. Leftover pastry can be made into small jelly tartlets, which are surprisingly popular with young-at-heart adults and children alike.

1 recipe whole wheat pie crust (page 24)
1 lb. ripe strawberries, halved
small fresh mint leaves

for the glaze
1/2 cup sugar
1/4 cup cornstarch
1 cup water
1/4 cup strawberry preserves
1 tbsp. lemon juice

Preheat oven to 400°F. Lightly butter a 9-inch tart pan. Roll out the pie crust on a floured surface, use it to line the tart pan, and chill for 20 minutes. Line the base of the pie crust with parchment weighted down with pie weights or baking beans, then bake for 12 minutes. Reduce the heat to 250°F and bake for 10 minutes more. Remove the parchment and beans and cook for another 10 minutes for the crust to dry out. Cool.

To make the glaze, mix together all the glaze ingredients in a saucepan. Bring to a boil and cook, stirring for 1 minute, until thickened. Remove from heat and cool slightly.

Spread half of the warm glaze over the cooked crust. Top with the strawberries, then brush the remaining warm glaze over the strawberries. Let cool and serve cold, garnished with small mint leaves.

Serves 6–8

variations

silken chocolate mousse

see base recipe page 231

chocolate mousse French-style
Prepare the basic recipe, using 2 tablespoons cognac in place of
the amaretto.

chocolate orange mousse
Prepare the basic recipe, using 3 tablespoons grand marnier, triple sec, or
orange juice in place of the amaretto and vanilla.

chocolate mousse dip with pineapple and strawberries
Prepare the basic recipe. Serve warm as a dip for chunks of pineapple and
whole strawberries.

peanut butter chocolate mousse pie
Prepare the basic recipe. Take one small prepared tart base, spread with a
thin layer of peanut butter, and top with the chocolate mousse.

chocolate truffles
Prepare the basic recipe, using 2 cups confectioners' sugar in place of the
maple syrup. Chill the mixture for 2 hours, then, working quickly, roll the
mixture into small balls. Roll them in cocoa powder, confectioners' sugar, or
shredded coconut. Drop truffles into candy cups to serve.

pistachio kulfi

see base recipe page 232

pistachio rosewater kulfi
Prepare the basic recipe, adding 2 tablespoons rosewater to the ingredients. Serve sprinkled with a few drops of rosewater and garnished with edible rose petals.

mango kulfi
Prepare the basic recipe, using only 1 tablespoon pistachios, ground to a powder, and adding the finely chopped flesh from 1 ripe mango to the mixture.

saffron almond kulfi
Prepare the basic recipe, using 1 cup blanched almonds in place of the pistachios. Add a pinch of saffron to the mixture and serve garnished with chopped pistachios.

malai kulfi
Prepare the basic recipe, omitting the pistachios.

variations

apple strudel

see base recipe page 234

apple & cranberry strudel
Prepare the basic recipe, using dried cranberries in place of the golden raisins.

apple & pear strudel
Prepare the basic recipe, using 2 apples and 2 pears.

apple & plum strudel
Prepare the basic recipe, using 2 apples and 4 roughly chopped, medium-sized plums. (The plum pieces do not need to wait in the acidulated water.)

peach & cardamom strudel
Prepare the basic recipe, using 4 large, peeled and pitted, ripe peaches in place of the apples (the peach slices do not need to wait in the acidulated water). Omit the golden raisins and use 1 teaspoon ground cardamom in place of the cinnamon.

baked rice pudding

see base recipe page 235

caribbean coconut rice pudding
Prepare the basic recipe, using 1 1/2 cups coconut milk and 2 1/2 cups soy milk. Add 2 tablespoons raisins and 2 tablespoons flaked coconut with the rice.

chocolate rice pudding
Prepare the basic recipe, using chocolate soy milk in place of the unsweetened soy milk. Use a little of this milk to mix with 2 tablespoons unsweetened cocoa powder to form a paste, then add it to the rice.

egyptian rice pudding
Prepare the basic recipe, using the lemon zest option. To the rice, add 2 lightly crushed cardamom pods, a pinch of saffron, and 2 tablespoons rosewater.

caramel rice pudding
Combine 3 tablespoons sugar and 3 tablespoons water in a small pan and cook gently, stirring, until dissolved; increase the heat slightly and continue to cook, without stirring, until a golden caramel is formed. Do not overcook; brown caramel is bitter. Immediately stir in 1 cup of the soy milk (be careful, as it will splatter), pour mixture into the prepared dish, and continue as with the basic recipe.

variations

tropical fruit kebabs

see base recipe page 236

orchard fruit kebabs
Prepare the basic recipe, replacing the tropical fruit with 1 large apple and 1 large pear, chopped into 1-inch chunks and coated with lemon juice, and 6 halved plums.

tropical fruit & bagel kebabs
Prepare the basic recipe. Cut a bagel in half and spread with nondairy butter, then sprinkle with brown sugar and cinnamon. Cut each bagel half into 6 pieces and thread them on the skewers with the fruit.

tropical fruit kebabs with orange cinnamon syrup
Prepare the basic recipe, adding 2 tablespoons orange juice concentrate in place of the vanilla in the syrup.

tropical fruit kebabs with chocolate sauce
Prepare the basic kebabs, and serve with chocolate sauce (page 239).

chocolate chip soy ice cream with hot chocolate sauce

see base recipe page 239

double chocolate chip soy ice cream with hot chocolate sauce
Prepare the basic recipe. Mix 1/4 cup cocoa powder to a paste with a little of the soy milk and add to the pan with the remaining soy milk. When cool, add 1 cup semisweet vegan chocolate chips.

peppermint chocolate chip soy ice cream with hot chocolate sauce
Prepare the basic recipe for double chocolate chip soy ice cream (above), using 1 tablespoon peppermint extract in place of the vanilla.

strawberry soy ice cream
Prepare the basic recipe, adding 1 1/2 cups crushed strawberries with the vanilla. The same principle applies for other berries and for mango or peach ice cream. Serve alone, or if desired, with the chocolate sauce.

banana "milkshake"
Prepare the basic recipe, omitting the sauce. Put in a blender 1 cup ice-cold soy or coconut milk, 4 scoops of vanilla soy ice cream (see variation above), 1 thickly sliced banana, and 1/2 teaspoon vanilla extract; blend until smooth.

variations

caramelized apple crisp

see base recipe page 240

caramelized peach crisp
Prepare the basic recipe, using 5 medium, ripe peaches in place of the apples. Add 1 tablespoon rum with the peaches for extra flavor.

caramelized apple ginger crisp
Prepare the basic recipe, adding 3 tablespoons chopped crystallized ginger to the apple mixture.

caramelized apple biscuit bake
Prepare the apples for the basic recipe. Make biscuits (page 133), using 1 tablespoon sugar in place of the rosemary. Arrange the biscuits on top of the apples and bake as directed.

caramelized apple crepe
Prepare the apples for the basic recipe. Make a batch of crepes (page 126). Stuff the crepes with the apples, arrange in an greased baking dish, and bake at 425° for 20 minutes, or until golden.

variations

toffeed banana with coconut cream

see base recipe page 241

toffeed pineapple with coconut cream
Prepare the basic recipe, using 8 slices fresh or canned pineapple in place of the bananas. Omit the lemon juice.

toffeed nectarines with coconut cream
Prepare the basic recipe, using 4 large, ripe nectarines, skinned, pitted, and halved, in place of the bananas.

red fruit salad with coconut cream
Prepare the coconut cream. To make the salad, combine 12 ounces cubed watermelon, 8 ounces strawberries, 4 ounces raspberries, the seeds from 1 pomegranate, and 2 chopped plums. Sprinkle with 1–2 tablespoons sugar and 1/4 cup cranberry juice and serve with the coconut cream.

asian fruit salad with coconut cream
Prepare the coconut cream. To make the salad: In a saucepan, dissolve 1/2 cup sugar in 2 cups water, bring to a boil, then add 1 star anise, 1 strip orange zest, and 1 split vanilla bean. Simmer until reduced by half; cool. Strain and pour over a salad made from 1/2 pineapple, 12 lychees, 1 papaya, 1 star fruit, and the pulp from a passion fruit. Serve with the coconut cream.

variations

no cheesecake with mixed berries

see base recipe page 242

pumpkin no cheesecake with maple syrup pecans
Prepare the basic recipe, adding 1 1/2 cups canned pumpkin purée to the tofu mixture. Replace the vanilla with 1 teaspoon ground cinnamon. For the topping, instead of the berries, toss 1 cup whole pecans with 3 tablespoons maple syrup, 1 tablespoon sugar, and 1/4 teaspoon cinnamon. Bake topping mixture at 350°F for 10 minutes; cool before using to decorate cheesecake.

no cheesecake with ginger & pineapple
Prepare the basic recipe, omitting topping. Add 1 teaspoon ground ginger to the graham cracker crumbs. Top the cheesecake with slices of fresh or canned pineapple and chopped crystallized ginger.

raspberry no cheesecake
Prepare the basic recipe, adding 1 cup raspberries to the mixture with the vanilla. Use 1 1/2 cups raspberries in place of the mixed berries for the topping.

chocolate no cheesecake
Prepare the basic recipe, replacing the graham crackers with Oreo cookies. To the filling, stir in 6 ounces vegan chocolate, melted, in place of the lemon juice and zest, and add 10 broken Oreo cookies.

variations

strawberry tart

see base recipe page 245

strawberry & cream tart
Prepare the basic recipe, halving the ingredients for the strawberry preserve glaze. Prepare one portion of nondairy whipped cream (page 21). Spread a very thin layer of glaze over the base of the tart to seal, then cover with the cream. Top with the strawberry halves, brush with the remaining warm glaze, and garnish with mint leaves.

blueberry tart
Prepare the basic recipe, using 1 pound fresh blueberries in place of the strawberries and blueberry preserve in place of the strawberry preserve.

french fruit tart
Prepare the basic recipe, replacing the strawberries with 1 pound mixed fresh strawberries, blueberries, raspberries, and peach slices. Heat 1/2 cup mixed fruit jelly with 2 tablespoons lemon juice until melted. Brush half this mixture over the base of the crust, arrange the fruit in concentric rings, then brush with remaining glaze. Omit the mint leaves.

baked goods

Baking without eggs does represent a challenge, but using a chemistry set of leavening agents and a selection of flours does the trick. The following recipes won't disappoint. The dairy-free fudge is an unexpected treat too!

raisin–walnut quick bread

see variations page 272

Quick breads are perfect for the lunchbox because they are best eaten the day after baking. This recipe uses ground flax seeds and walnuts, both of which are high in omega-3 fatty acids—good news for those avoiding fish oil supplements.

1 cup all-purpose flour
2 tsp. baking powder
1/4 tsp. salt
1 cup fine-milled whole wheat flour
1 cup raisins
3/4 cup sugar

1/2 cup slivered almonds
1 tsp. flax seed meal
1/4 cup water
1 tsp. orange zest
1/2 cup freshly squeezed orange juice
1/2 cup sunflower oil

Preheat oven to 350°F. Grease and flour a 9x5-inch loaf pan. In a large bowl, sift together the all-purpose flour, baking powder, and salt, then add the whole wheat flour. Toss in the raisins, coating them in flour to prevent them from sticking together and sinking while cooking. Stir in the sugar and almonds, and mix thoroughly.

In a small bowl, blend together the flax seed meal and water until white and foamy. Add the orange zest, orange juice, and sunflower oil. Stir the wet ingredients into the dry ingredients and mix until just blended, adding a little more orange juice or water if the mixture feels stiff; do not overmix.

Pour the batter into the prepared pan and bake for 60 minutes, or until the loaf is firm to the touch and a toothpick inserted into the center of the loaf comes out clean. Cool for 10 minutes before removing from the pan and cooling on a wire rack.
Makes 1 loaf

lemon–poppy seed cupcakes

see variations page 273

These cupcakes are delicious with a cup of tea. They have a bright, zingy taste accentuated by the strong crusty syrup on top. The lemon juice activates the baking soda, which makes these cupcakes rise so successfully and gives them a good texture.

2 1/4 cups all-purpose flour
2 tbsp. cornstarch
1 1/2 tsp. baking soda
3/4 tsp. salt
1/2 cup semolina or brown rice flour
1/4 cup poppy seeds
1 1/4 cups oat milk or other nondairy milk

1/2 cup (1 stick) soy margarine, melted
3/4 cup canola oil
1/4 cup freshly squeezed lemon juice
zest of 1 small lemon
for the lemon syrup
1/3 cup freshly squeezed lemon juice
1/3 cup sugar

Preheat oven to 350°F. Line a muffin pan with paper muffin cups. In a bowl, sift together the flour, cornstarch, baking soda, and salt. Stir in the semolina and poppy seeds. Make a well in the middle and pour in the milk, melted margarine, oil, and lemon juice. Use a wire whisk to combine. Stir in the lemon zest.

Pour the batter into the prepared baking cups to about 1/2 inch from the top. Bake for 20–25 minutes, until a toothpick inserted into the center comes out clean.

Meanwhile, stir together the lemon juice and sugar for the topping. When the cupcakes are done, stab them all over with a toothpick. Using a teaspoon, drizzle the syrup over the hot cupcakes, letting the syrup soak into them. Remove from the pan and cool on a wire rack.

Makes 12 cupcakes

chocolate brownies

see variations page 274

This brownie recipe is for those who like their brownies strongly chocolaty and soft and sticky in the middle with a slight crustiness on the top. Decadent or what?

1/3 cup soy margarine
3 (1-oz.) squares semisweet vegan chocolate
1/2 cup granulated sugar
1/2 cup brown sugar
1 tsp. vanilla extract

egg replacer for 2 eggs (page 24)
1/4 cup oat milk or other nondairy milk
3/4 cup all-purpose flour

Preheat oven to 350°F. Grease an 8x8-inch pan and line the base with parchment paper.

Melt the margarine and chocolate in a bowl placed over a saucepan of simmering water, stirring occasionally. Stir in the granulated sugar, brown sugar, and vanilla.

In a small bowl, whisk together the egg replacer and the oat milk until frothy. Pour into the chocolate mixture and stir. Sift in the flour and stir, just until all the ingredients are combined. Pour the batter into the prepared pan and bake for about 25 minutes, until the center of the brownies is just firm to touch and has set. Do not overcook; the brownies should be very soft. Allow to cool for 10 minutes, then remove from the pan and cut into pieces.

Makes 9–12 brownies

cranberry–orange oatmeal cookies

see variations page 275

These are great cookies, stuffed full of fruit and flavor. The baking soda is activated by the hot liquid, so it is best to work quickly to mix it into the batter and not to delay the cooking.

1 cup (2 sticks) soy margarine
1/2 cup brown sugar
1/2 cup white sugar
3/4 cup all-purpose flour, sifted
3/4 cup fine-milled whole wheat flour
1/2 tsp. salt

1/4 cup orange juice
1 tsp. baking soda
grated zest of 1 orange
2 cups quick-cooking oats
1 1/2 cups dried cranberries

Preheat oven to 350°F. Lightly grease 1 or 2 cookie sheets. In a large bowl, beat the margarine and the sugars until light and fluffy. Stir in the flours and salt. Bring the orange juice to a boil in a small saucepan, remove from the heat, and stir in the baking soda to dissolve. Quickly add the mixture to the bowl, along with the orange zest, oats, and cranberries.

Drop the mixture by teaspoonfuls for small cookies (or by tablespoonfuls for larger cookies) onto the cookie sheet, leaving space between them to allow them to spread. Cook for 10–12 minutes, until the edges become a light golden brown. Cool for 3 minutes, then transfer the cookies to a wire rack to cool completely. Repeat until all the cookie dough is used.

Makes 15–30 cookies

carrot cake with lemon frosting

see variations page 276

If you wish, you can use just whole wheat flour and brown sugar, but choose a finely milled whole wheat flour for best effect.

1 cup all-purpose flour, sifted
1 cup whole wheat flour
1/4 cup cornstarch
1 cup brown sugar
1/2 cup granulated sugar
1 1/2 tsp. ground cinnamon
egg replacer for 2 eggs (page 24)
1/4 cup orange juice
1 1/4 cups sunflower oil
1 cup soy milk

1 tbsp. cider vinegar
3 cups shredded carrots
1/2 cup golden raisins
1/2 cup chopped pecans or walnuts
for the frosting
4 oz. nondairy cream cheese
1/4 cup (1/2 stick) soy margarine, melted
1 tsp. vanilla extract
1 tsp. lemon juice
2–2 1/4 cups confectioners' sugar

Preheat oven to 350°F. Grease a 9x13-inch pan and line the base with parchment paper. Combine the flours, cornstarch, sugars, and cinnamon in a large bowl. In a separate bowl, mix the egg replacer with 2 tablespoons of the orange juice, and whisk with a fork until fluffy. Pour into the dry ingredients with the remaining orange juice, sunflower oil, soy milk, and cider vinegar. Mix thoroughly, ensuring that all the dry ingredients are moistened. Stir in the carrots, followed by the golden raisins and nuts. Pour the batter into the prepared pan. Bake for 40–50 minutes, until the cake feels firm to the touch and a toothpick inserted into the center comes out clean. Cool for 10 minutes before turning out onto a wire rack to cool completely. To make the frosting: Beat the nondairy cream cheese until soft and smooth, then stir in the melted margarine, vanilla, and lemon juice. Sift in the confectioners' sugar until the frosting has a spreadable consistency. Spread over the rectangular cake.
Serves 4

banana cake & passion fruit glaze

see variations page 277

Banana cake goes well with the bold taste of passion fruit — vegan cakes needn't be dull!

3 large ripe bananas
1/4 cup sunflower oil
1/4 cup oat milk
1/2 cup brown sugar
1 tbsp. rum or 1 tsp. vanilla extract
egg replacer for 1 egg (page 24)
1 tbsp. water
1 1/2 cups fine-milled whole wheat flour
1 tsp. baking powder

1 tsp. salt
1/4 tsp. ground cinnamon
1/4 tsp. ground nutmeg
1/2 cup chopped walnuts

for the passion fruit glaze
1/3 cup passion fruit pulp
1/3 cup brown rice syrup or light corn syrup
1 tbsp. brown sugar

Preheat oven to 350°F. Oil an 8 1/2 x 4 1/2-inch loaf pan. Line the base with parchment. Mash the bananas in a bowl and immediately stir in the oil, oat milk, brown sugar, and rum or vanilla. In a cup, whisk the egg replacer and the water with a fork until frothy. In a separate bowl, combine the flour, baking powder, salt, cinnamon, and nutmeg. Pour the banana mixture and the egg replacer into the flour mixture and stir until well combined. Add the walnuts. Pour the batter into the prepared pan. Bake for 55-60 minutes until firm to the touch and a toothpick inserted into the center comes out clean. Cool for 10 minutes, then turn out and cool completely on a wire rack. For the glaze, combine the passion fruit pulp, syrup, and sugar in a small saucepan. Cook over a gentle heat until the sugar has dissolved. Increase the heat, bring to a boil, and cook, without stirring, for about 2 minutes, until the mixture has thickened slightly. Remove from heat. The glaze will continue to thicken as it cools. When the cake and glaze are fully cooled, spread the glaze over the cake.

Serves 8–12

high-energy cookies

see variations page 278

These cookies are great for lunchboxes or to take on a hike. If it is going to be a hot day, omit the carob drizzle on the top.

1/4 cup (1/2 stick) soy margarine
1/4 cup unsweetened applesauce
3/4 cup brown sugar
1/3 cup crunchy peanut butter
1 cup all-purpose flour
1 tsp. baking soda
1/2 tsp. salt
egg replacer for 1 egg (page 24)

1 tbsp. water
1 tsp. vanilla extract
1/2 cup quick-cooking oats
1 cup mixed dried fruit (raisins and chopped
    apricots, prunes, and/or figs)
1/4 cup pumpkin seeds
2 (1-oz.) squares vegan semisweet carob

Preheat oven to 350°F. Lightly grease 1 or 2 cookie sheets. In a bowl, beat together the margarine, applesauce, brown sugar, and peanut butter. In a separate bowl, sift together the flour, baking soda, and salt. In a cup, mix the egg replacer with the water and whisk with a fork until frothy. Stir the dry ingredients and the egg replacer into the margarine mixture. Add the vanilla, oats, dried fruit, and pumpkin seeds.

Drop the dough by tablespoonfuls onto the cookie sheets, leaving space between them to allow them to spread. Cook for 10–12 minutes, until the edges become a light golden brown. Cool for 3 minutes, then transfer to a wire rack. Repeat until all the dough is used. Once the cookies are cool, melt the carob and drizzle it on top of the cookies.

Makes 15–18 cookies

lavender-dusted lemon shortbread

see variations page 279

Lavender sugar is available to purchase, but you can make your own by making a lavender bag from a small handful of lavender petals sewn into a small cotton pouch. Put this into a jar containing 1 cup sugar and leave it for 2 weeks, shaking occasionally.

1 1/2 cups all-purpose flour	1 cup (2 sticks) soy margarine or
1/2 cup cornstarch	nondairy butter
pinch salt	zest of 1 lemon
1/2 cup superfine sugar	2–3 tbsp. lavender sugar, to dust

Preheat oven to 300°F. Lightly grease a cookie sheet. Put the flour, cornstarch, and salt into a food processor, and pulse a few times to sift and combine. Cut the margarine or nondairy butter into chunks and add to the flour with the sugar and lemon zest. Pulse until the fat is fully incorporated. If making the dough without a food processor, rub the margarine or nondairy butter into the flour, cornstarch, and salt; then add the sugar and lemon zest.

Turn the mixture out onto a lightly floured work surface and knead together into a dough. Roll out into a circle about 1/3 inch thick and crimp the edges either with your thumb and forefinger or with a fork. Prick the surface of the shortbread all over with a fork and mark into 8 wedges. Alternatively, press the dough into a 1/3-inch-thick rectangle, prick all over, and mark into fingers. Transfer the dough onto the cookie sheet and bake for about 25 minutes until very lightly golden at the edges. Cool for 5 minutes before cutting into segments and transferring to a wire rack to cool completely. Dust with the lavender sugar.

Makes 8 shortbread cookies

chocolate cake with glossy frosting

see variations page 280

This is such a decadent chocolate cake — even your non-vegan guests will be surprised.

1 cup raw sugar
1/3 cup shortening, at room temperature
1 1/2 cups all-purpose flour, sifted, or whole
    wheat flour
1/4 cup unsweetened cocoa powder
1 tsp. baking soda
1/4 tsp. baking powder
1/2 tsp. salt
1 cup cold water
1 tbsp. cider vinegar

1 tsp. vanilla extract
for the frosting
3 tbsp. shortening
3 (1-oz.) squares vegan semisweet chocolate
1/3 cup soy milk
1 tsp. vanilla extract
1/4 tsp. salt
2 cups confectioners' sugar
chopped pistachio or macadamia nuts,
    to decorate

Preheat oven to 350°F. Grease 2 (8-inch) round pans and line the bases with parchment paper. Combine the sugar and shortening in a bowl or food processor and beat to combine — the mixture will look like crumbs. Add all the remaining cake ingredients and beat well. Divide the batter between the prepared cake pans and bake for 25–35 minutes, or until the cakes feel firm to the touch and a toothpick inserted into the center comes out clean. Cool for 5 minutes, then turn out onto a wire rack to cool completely.

To make the frosting, melt the shortening and chocolate in a bowl placed over a saucepan of simmering water. Stir occasionally. Remove the bowl from the heat and stir in the milk, vanilla, and salt. Sift in the confectioners' sugar until the frosting is of spreading consistency. Use to sandwich the cakes together, then spread the remainder on top and side of the cake. Decorate with chopped pistachio or macadamia nuts.
Makes 12 slices

vanilla fudge

see variations page 281

This fudge makes a terrific gift for vegans and anyone on a dairy-free diet. Give it to nonvegans, and they will express surprise. They never thought vegans could have it so good!

1 1/2 cups soy milk
1 cup sugar

1/2 cup (1 stick) nondairy butter or margarine
2 tsp. vanilla extract

Grease a 7x7-inch baking pan and line it with parchment. Put the soy milk, sugar, and nondairy butter or margarine in a very large pan — the mixture expands considerably while boiling. Insert a candy thermometer, and cook over a moderate heat until the sugar has dissolved. Bring to a boil, cover, and cook for 3 minutes.

Remove the cover and continue to simmer for 15–20 minutes, stirring constantly, until a candy thermometer reaches 270°F (soft ball stage). (If you do not have a candy thermometer, drop a little of the mixture into a cup of cold water. It will form into a soft ball when it is hot enough; until then it will just disperse in the water.) It is extremely important to stir continuously throughout this process, as fudge can easily scorch.

Remove the fudge from the heat immediately and put the base of the pan into a bowl of cold water to cool quickly and stop the cooking process. Stir in the vanilla and beat until the mixture thickens and loses its gloss. Pour into the prepared baking pan and put on a wire rack. When almost set, mark into 1-inch squares. When it has cooled and set completely, cut into pieces. Arrange in a decorative box or in plastic bags tied with raffia ribbon.

Makes 49 pieces

raisin–walnut quick bread

see base recipe page 257

date–walnut quick bread
Prepare the basic recipe, using chopped dates in place of the raisins.

cranberry–pecan quick bread
Prepare the basic recipe, using dried cranberries in place of the raisins and pecans in place of the walnuts.

cherry–almond quick bread
Prepare the basic recipe, using roughly chopped dried cherries in place of the raisins and flaked almonds in place of the walnuts.

zucchini quick bread
Prepare the basic recipe, replacing the raisins with 2 cups grated zucchini, 1 teaspoon ground cinnamon, and 1/2 teaspoon baking soda.

lemon poppy seed cupcakes

see base recipe page 258

lemon & lime poppy seed cupcakes
Prepare the basic cupcake recipe, using the zest of 1/2 lemon and 1/2 lime in place of the lemon zest. In both the cake and the syrup, use 2 tablespoons lemon juice and 2 tablespoons lime juice in place of the lemon juice.

orange poppy seed cupcakes
Prepare the basic cupcake recipe, using 1/4 cup orange juice and the zest of 1/2 large orange in place of the lemon juice and zest. In the syrup, use 3 tablespoons orange juice and 1 tablespoon lemon juice.

lemon almond cupcakes
Prepare the basic recipe, using 1/4 cup ground almonds in place of the poppy seeds.

orange almond cupcakes
Prepare the orange poppy seed cupcakes (above). Additionally, use 1/4 cup ground almonds in place of the poppy seeds.

variations

chocolate brownies

see base recipe page 260

hot chocolate brownies
Prepare the basic recipe. Serve as soon as the brownies are cut into pieces, accompanied by chocolate chip vegan or vanilla "ice cream" (page 239).

chocolate almond brownies
Prepare the basic recipe, adding 1/2 cup flaked almonds and a few drops of almond extract to the batter.

chocolate chip brownies
Prepare the basic recipe, adding 1/2 cup vegan semisweet chocolate chips to the batter.

whole wheat chocolate chip brownies
Prepare the basic recipe, using whole wheat flour in place of all-purpose flour and substituting brown sugar for the white sugar. Add 2 extra tablespoons soy milk to the batter.

cranberry-orange oatmeal cookies

see base recipe page 261

cranberry-pecan oatmeal cookies
Prepare the basic mixture, using 1/4 cup boiling water in place of the orange
juice, 1 teaspoon vanilla extract in place of the orange zest, and 3/4 cup
chopped pecans in place of 3/4 cup of the dried cranberries.

raisin-pecan oatmeal cookies
Prepare the cranberry and pecan variation above, but use raisins in place of the
cranberries.

chocolate chip-orange oatmeal cookies
Prepare the basic recipe, using 1 1/2 cups vegan semisweet chocolate chips or
chopped vegan chocolate in place of the cranberries.

blueberry-orange oatmeal cookies
Prepare the basic recipe, using 1 1/2 cups fresh blueberries in place of the dried
cranberries. (Blueberries work well in the cranberry pecan oat variation too,
using 3/4 cup blueberries in place of the cranberries.)

carrot cake with lemon frosting

see base recipe page 262

carrot & pineapple cake with lemon frosting
Prepare the basic recipe, replacing half the shredded carrots with 1 1/2 cups well-drained crushed pineapple.

carrot & zucchini cake with lemon frosting
Prepare the basic recipe, replacing half the shredded carrots with 1 1/2 cups shredded zucchini.

carrot cake with passion fruit glaze
Prepare the basic carrot cake, but replace the frosting with a double quantity of passion fruit glaze (page 265).

carrot cake with lemon-coconut frosting
Prepare the basic recipe. Lightly toast 3/4 cup shredded coconut under a medium-hot broiler until the edges become lightly golden – watch carefully as it quickly burns. Cool and lightly press into the frosting.

banana cake & passion fruit glaze

see base recipe page 265

banana cake & chocolate chips
Prepare the basic recipe, using 3/4 cup vegan semisweet chocolate chips or chopped vegan chocolate in place of the walnuts. Sprinkle 2 tablespoons brown sugar (a crystalline sugar such as demerara is good) over the top of the cake before baking. Omit the glaze.

banana & orange cake with passion fruit glaze
Prepare the basic recipe, using 2 tablespoons orange juice, the zest of 1 orange, and 1 teaspoon lemon juice in place of the rum or vanilla extract.

banana raisin cake & passion fruit glaze
Prepare the basic recipe, adding 3/4 cup raisins to the batter.

banana almond cake & passion fruit glaze
Prepare the basic recipe, replacing 1/4 cup of the whole wheat flour with 1/4 cup ground almonds. Also, use 1/2 cup chopped blanched almonds in place of the walnuts.

variations

high-energy cookies

see base recipe page 266

gluten-free high-energy cookies
Prepare the basic recipe, using gluten-free flour in place of the all-purpose flour. Add 1-2 tablespoons soy milk to the mixture if it feels stiff (gluten-free flours tend to be drier than wheat flours).

carob high-energy cookies
Prepare the basic recipe, using only 2/3 cup mixed fruit and adding 1/3 cup vegan carob chips to the dough.

granola carob cookies
Prepare the basic recipe, using 1 1/4 cups granola and 1/2 cup carob chips in place of the oats, mixed fruit, and pumpkin seeds.

almond apricot high-energy cookies
Prepare the basic recipe, using almond butter in place of the peanut butter. Use 3/4 cup chopped dried apricots in place of the mixed fruit and 1/2 cup chopped blanched almonds in place of the pumpkin seeds.

lavender-dusted lemon shortbread

see base recipe page 267

traditional scottish shortbread
Prepare the basic recipe, using 1 cup all-purpose flour plus 1/2 cup rice flour and omitting the lemon zest. Dust with superfine sugar instead of lavender sugar.

ginger shortbread
Prepare the basic recipe, using 1/4 cup finely chopped crystallized ginger in place of the lemon zest. Dust with superfine sugar instead of lavender sugar.

lavender-dusted pecan shortbread
Prepare the basic recipe, using 1/3 cup finely chopped pecans in place of the lemon zest.

chocolate chip shortbread
Prepare the basic recipe, using 1/3 cup vegan semisweet chocolate chips in place of the lemon zest. There is no need to dust these cookies with additional sugar after cooking.

variations

chocolate cake with glossy frosting

see base recipe page 268

carob cake with glossy frosting
Prepare the basic recipe, using carob powder in place of the cocoa powder in the cake. Use carob in place of chocolate in the frosting.

mocha cake with glossy frosting
Prepare the basic recipe, using 2 teaspoons instant coffee with the cocoa. Add 1 teaspoon instant coffee to the frosting.

chocolate cupcakes
Prepare the basic recipe. Pour the batter into paper liners in a cupcake pan. Fill to about 1/2 inch from the top of the liners, then bake for 20–25 minutes until a toothpick inserted into the cupcake centers comes out clean. Cool, then use the frosting to decorate the individual cupcakes.

chocolate sponge pudding
Prepare a half portion of the basic cake recipe and bake it in a 7-inch ovenproof dish that has been greased and lined with parchment paper. Allow to cool for 5 minutes, turn out onto a plate, and serve hot with vanilla vegan "ice cream" (page 239). Omit the frosting.

vanilla fudge

see base recipe page 271

chocolate fudge
Prepare the basic recipe, using just 1 teaspoon vanilla extract. Stir the vanilla and 4 (1-ounce) squares vegan semisweet chocolate into the mixture at the same time.

mocha fudge
Prepare the chocolate fudge variation above, but use 2 teaspoons instant coffee in place of the 2 teaspoons vanilla extract.

vanilla cherry fudge
Prepare the basic recipe, stirring in 1/3 cup chopped candied cherries to the mixture at the same time as the vanilla.

rum raisin fudge
Prepare the basic recipe, using 1/2 cup plump raisins and 2 tablespoons rum in place of the vanilla.

nutty almond fudge
Prepare the basic recipe, using 1/3 cup roughly chopped toasted almonds and a few drops of almond extract in place of the vanilla.

index